Obligation and Opportunity:
Single Maritime Women in Boston, 1870–1930

In the years between Confederation and the Depression nearly 500,000 Maritimers left their homes to work in the United States or other parts of Canada. Why they left and how their departure affected the region's economy have long been debated but, until now, a major component of that exodus has been largely ignored. In *Obligation and Opportunity* Betsy Beattie addresses this oversight, examining the lives of the tens of thousands of single Maritime women who left to work in Boston between 1870 and 1930.

Carefully crafted from oral interviews, diaries, letters, written recollections, census data, and other historical sources, *Obligation and Opportunity* opens a window into the world of the women who moved from the Maritimes to New England for work. Urged to stay home by tales of danger and woe in the newspapers, they still left by the thousands, and in numbers larger than those for men.

Beattie examines the rural families they left, the urban environment they entered in Boston, and the different occupations they filled. She sheds new light on the response of rural families to economic change and on the effects of gender on choices for young women. She demonstrates that first-generation emigrants, who left out of a need to find work and send money back home, eased the way for second-generation emigrants, who left to seek opportunities in the big city.

Obligation and Opportunity offers new insights not only for everyone interested in the history of the Maritimes and Boston but also for scholars and others interested in family history, women's studies, labour history, and migration studies.

BETSY BEATTIE is the Canadian studies librarian at the University of Maine.

Obligation and Opportunity

Single Maritime Women in Boston, 1870–1930

BETSY BEATTIE

McGill-Queen's University Press
Montreal & Kingston · London · Ithaca

© McGill-Queen's University Press 2000
ISBN 0-7735-2018-x (cloth)
ISBN 0-7735-2019-8 (paper)

Legal deposit first quarter 2000
Bibliothèque nationale du Québec

Printed in Canada on acid-free paper

This book has been published with the help of a grant from the Canadian-American Center of the University of Maine.

McGill-Queen's University Press acknowledges the financial support of the Government of Canada through the Book Publishing Industry Development Program (BPIDP) for its activities. We also acknowledge the support of the Canada Council for the Arts for our publishing program.

Canadian Cataloguing in Publication Data

Beattie, Mary Elizabeth, 1945–
    Obligation and opportunity : single Maritime women in Boston, 1870–1930
    Includes bibliographical references and index.
    ISBN 0-7735-2018-x (bound) – ISBN 0-7735-2019-8 (pbk.)
    1. Single women – Employment – Massachusetts – Boston – History – 19th century. 2. Single women – Employment – Massachusetts – Boston – History – 20th century. 3. Single women – Maritime Provinces – Economic conditions. I. Title.
    HD6096.B7B43 2000   331.4'09744'6109034   C99-900859-5

Typeset in Palatino 10/12
by Caractéra inc., Quebec City

Contents

Tables and Figures

FIGURES

Illustrations

Acknowledgments

This study, like all historical writing, is the product of collaboration. It is built on the research, findings, and ideas of scholars from North America and Europe, who deserve mention beyond citations in the text. To them, and others, whose works have consciously or unconsciously inspired my thinking, I am indebted. In addition, there are individuals and institutions to whom I owe a special word of thanks.

At various stages in my research I depended upon the guidance and knowledge of staff members at numerous libraries and archives in Canada and the United States. The Provincial Archives of New Brunswick, the Nova Scotia Archives and Records Management, the Public Archives and Records Office of Prince Edward Island, the Archives of Dalhousie University, and the Nursing Archives in the Mugar Library at Boston University deserve particular mention. With limited time and a confusing array of censuses, vital statistics, manuscripts, and photographs to view, I appreciated the patient help of their reference staffs and the backstage work of those who organized the materials for easy access. I owe a special debt of gratitude to Harry Holman, at the archives in Prince Edward Island, who spent many hours broadening my knowledge of Island history.

I would also like to thank scholars who offered me their time, thoughts, materials, and direction. David Weale at the University of Prince Edward Island shared his own and his students' insights on out-migration. Ian McKay at Queen's University generously allowed me to consult his file of citations from Maritime newspapers, saving me hundreds of hours of research. Rusty Bittermann, Margaret Conrad, and Gwendolyn Davies all encouraged me and influenced my thinking at various stages of my research. Among the faculty members at the University of Maine who offered assistance, I am particularly grateful to Sandy Ives, whose training module on oral interviewing teaches human respect as well as technical skills, and to Stephen Hornsby, who brought his own knowledge of Maritime out-migration to a reading of my study and encouraged me to consider submitting the manuscript for publication. Finally, I offer a sincere thanks to Robert Babcock, who guided the creation of this work from its inception to its final revisions. His suggestions were indispensable, but even more valuable has been his unflagging support for my work.

I am grateful, as well, to the Canadian-American Center at the University of Maine for its financial support. From the beginning of the project, I received travel grants from the center to do research in the Maritimes and to present papers at conferences, where I received valuable critiques from other historians. And when the work was completed, the center generously covered the costs required for its publication. For this support I again thank Stephen Hornsby, director of the Canadian-American Center and enthusiastic champion of Canadian scholarship at the University of Maine.

Reflecting on all those who contributed to this endeavour, I reserve my deepest gratitude for a group of people, most of whom I have never met. These are the over fifty individuals who answered my newspaper inquiries about women from the Maritimes who went to work in New England. Sons, daughters, nieces, nephews, grandchildren, and some of the women migrants themselves responded to my request. The result was an outpouring of stories, letters, memoirs, diaries, photographs, and personal interviews that, taken together, form the body of my research. Such interest, time, and openness with a total stranger was a moving testimony to the kindness and generosity of these individuals. It is to them that I dedicate this book.

Obligation and Opportunity

Introduction:
The Unfinished History of
Maritime Out-migration

Newspapers sounded the alarm. "What shall we do," lamented the Halifax *Herald* in its headline of 31 December 1904, "to keep our young men in Nova Scotia?"[1] The Amherst *Daily News* of 3 October 1898 cautioned: "In a letter ... recently received from Boston it is stated that there is so large an influx of young girls from the blue-nose land that wages of those who go to live out at service are greatly reduced."[2] A popular song of the 1880s told the same story:

> The Father's boy, his only joy,
> Must bid a sad farewell;
> They're parting here, no more to meet
> On earth, for who can tell ...
>
> Our daughters fair, in deep despair,
> Must leave their native land;
> To foreign shores they're swiftly borne,
> As I do understand ...
>
> Prince Edward Isle adieu.[3]

Throughout the Maritime provinces in the years between Confederation and the Great Depression the citizenry worried about the future of their region because so many among them – mostly young, single men and women – were leaving home to find work and take up residence elsewhere.[4]

Statistics of population movement give foundation to these fears. According to figures in Alan Brookes's dissertation "The Exodus," 308,000 residents of the Maritime provinces left the region between 1871 and 1901, a figure that represented 41 percent of its 1871 population.[5] In a 1960 study of population changes in the Atlantic provinces Kari Levitt estimated that New Brunswick, Nova Scotia, and Prince Edward Island suffered a net out-migration of 341,000 persons between 1881 and 1921 while the rest of Canada experienced a net in-migration of over 750,000.[6] More recent research places the region's net loss of population between the 1860s and 1920s at nearly 500,000.[7]

THE HISTORIOGRAPHY OF OUT-MIGRATION AND THE MARITIME ECONOMY

Scholars writing about Maritime out-migration may disagree about numbers, but they share a common focus for their discussion: the relationship between the region's depopulation and its economic decline.[8] The most common explanation for out-migration, posed first by Marcus Hansen and J. Bartlet Brebner and more fully developed by Alan Brookes, stressed that the failure of the Maritime provinces to sustain their declining shipbuilding, fishing, and farming economies, or to replace them with a vigorous industrial sector, caused a younger generation of skilled labourers and farmers to seek jobs elsewhere. Hansen and Brebner, in *The Mingling of the Canadian and American Peoples*, described surplus farm workers and apprentice craftsmen heading to the United States to pursue "fishing, lumbering, manufacturing in the East, agriculture in the West."[9] In "The Exodus" Alan Brookes made the cause-and-effect relationship between economic change and out-migration more explicit. He revealed the high rate of population loss from those communities like Canning, Nova Scotia, that had been dependent on the Maritime "wood, wind, and sail" economy, had failed to develop technologically advanced industries, and were bypassed by new rail transportation routes.[10]

In the introduction to *Away*, an oral history of Maritime emigrants, Gary Burrill offered a different economic explanation for out-migration from the region, one based on the work of Henry Veltmeyer. Veltmeyer, in an article entitled "The Capitalist Underdevelopment of Atlantic Canada," argued that the Maritime provinces, poorer and more peripheral parts of Canada than Ontario and Quebec, were victims of exploitation and purposeful underdevelopment by wealthy and powerful capitalists of central Canada, in much the same way that Latin American countries have been exploited by capitalists in North America. Financiers of Montreal and Toronto took over Maritime industries, banks, and transportation systems, driving local enterprises out of business. They extracted the region's natural resources such as coal but built plants to manufacture finished goods in central Canada. The region's human resources, left without local employment, were forced to look for work outside the Maritimes, adding to the labour pool in more industrialized areas and helping to keep wages low.[11] In Burrill's view, Maritime emigrants, whether they resettled in central Canada, the Canadian West, or the United States, were the unwitting victims of this process of capitalist underdevelopment.[12]

Patricia Thornton, in "The Problem of Out-migration from Atlantic Canada, 1871–1921," also connected the region's economic problems to out-migration, but in a novel way. Noting that sustained economic decline in the Maritimes did not begin until the 1890s, while out-migration began as early as the 1860s, Thornton presented the relationship in reverse: the loss of young, talented workers from the Maritimes led, in turn, to the failure of the region to develop a strong economy.[13] Since the Maritime region was not in desperate economic straits when out-migration began, Thornton argued that "pull" factors such as jobs in cities or land in the West convinced the young to emigrate, and that those who left were a disproportionately skilled part of the population.[14] While she did not explain how the pre-industrial skills of Maritime emigrants would have been useful in building an industrial economy, she did demonstrate that a sizeable part of the out-migration process predated the worst years of regional stagnation and decline.[15]

Thus, a historical debate has developed over the cause-and-effect relationship between out-migration and economic change in the Maritimes. However, at the root of the controversy is an assumption shared by all parties to the debate: that the young people who left the region deprived it of skilled workers – the "painters, blacksmiths, carpenters, and shoemakers" – who might have built a stronger Maritime economy had they remained.[16] Implicit in that reasoning is the assumption that these emigrants were male.

Yet statistics from these historians' own research contradict this assumption. Patricia Thornton, for example, wrote that "females appear to have had a greater propensity to leave the region than men," a fact corroborated by net migration figures from 1871 to 1891 for each of the three provinces.[17] Alan Brookes, although focusing his study on male heads of households, noted that women outnumbered men approximately two to one among single immigrants in Boston in 1880.[18] One of Thornton's findings helps explain the predominance of single women in Boston. "The immigration to the frontier was predominately male-led and relatively less age selective," she observed, "while cityward immigration was heavily female-led and highly concentrated among the young, single age-group."[19]

The fact that, at least until 1890, the majority of emigrants from the Maritimes were women does not necessarily weaken the argument that out-migration and economic change were related. Rather, it demonstrates the limiting effect of studying out-migration only in terms of declining economic opportunity for men. In such a study the experiences of over half of those who left are overlooked or misunderstood. For example, Brookes mentioned Maritime women only briefly, noting their predilection for domestic service, because he was mainly concerned with the uprooted Maritime "shipbuilders and carpenters."[20] Hansen and Brebner also mentioned Maritime "girls" working as domestics in Boston but then listed occupations such as farming, lumbering, and manufacturing as the primary job choices of Maritimers in the United States.[21] Only Thornton considered the importance of women, claiming that the loss of single women undermined industrial growth because "it is now widely agreed that the Industrial Revolution was built on the backs of the cheap labour of women."[22] However, her argument ignored Alan Brookes's findings that those same women, once in Boston, overwhelmingly chose domestic service over factory work.[23]

Thus, the core of historical literature on Maritime out-migration, constrained by a narrow focus on regional economic decline, offers an inadequate, male-centred explanation of the phenomenon. The lives of female emigrants remain largely unexplored in spite of statistics indicating the large numbers of such women in the migrant stream. Without this component the history of the Maritimes "exodus" is incomplete.

There is some encouraging evidence that the male-only perspective on Maritime out-migration is changing. In 1994 Fiona Bellerive wrote a Masters thesis examining the important role that the Young Women's Christian Association (YWCA) of Boston played in the lives of many female migrants to New England's largest city. At once a welcoming haven for new arrivals, an employment agency, a place to board, and a source of moral guidance rooted in evangelical Protestantism, the YWCA offered a range of institutional support services to Maritime women living and working in Boston.[24] In Bellerive's words, the Boston YWCA was one of the major "systems of power" with which these women contended: it negotiated between the needs of young migrant women and the concerns of the native-born middle classes who worried about moral decay born of rapid urban immigration even as they welcomed the prospect of an increased pool of domestic servants from "the provinces."[25]

Bellerive's study is a welcome addition to the literature, introducing Maritime women into the larger discussion of "the exodus." However, its twenty-year span and its focus on specific aspects of the migrant experience in the city leave several issues of female out-migration unexplored. These gaps include not only the living and working conditions of Maritime women in Boston but also their relationships to families in the Maritimes, their reasons for leaving home, and how these reasons may have changed over the six decades of greatest emigration from the region. In general, there is still much historical work to do to connect single Maritime women emigrants to the world they left.

Although existing research on Maritime out-migration does not adequately explain why women left the region, a growing body of historical literature on the Maritimes lays the groundwork for a fresh approach to the issue of emigration that addresses gender differences as well as the relationship of emigrants to economic conditions back home. Works by T.W. Acheson, Rusty Bittermann, Robert MacKinnon, Graeme Wynn, Danny Samson, and Steven Maynard have examined the rural economy of the Maritime provinces in different periods of the nineteenth century by studying communities in depth to unearth details of economic life, often at the family level.[26] The locales examined – Hopewell, Hardwood Hill, Middle River, and Inverness in Nova Scotia and St David's and Wakefield parishes in New Brunswick – do not cover the full geography of the region. However, the studies all explore the nature of pre-industrial economic life in agricultural regions; and since the most common occupation of Maritimers throughout much of the nineteenth century was farming, it is likely that the findings for these communities applied to a large proportion of the Maritime population.[27]

The economic realities these historians found in the communities studied were strikingly similar: inequalities among the farm households of a region, with a small percentage of families reaping consistent profits from their harvests and other investments and a far larger percentage unable to support themselves solely from farm production. For some farm households, dependence on outside help or wages from off-farm work was an annual need; for others, just a sporadic one. Still, profitable, even subsistence, farming was an unrealized goal for all but a few rural households.[28] From such conditions emerged the pattern of multiple occupations so common in the rural regions of the Maritimes – the farmer who worked for part of the year in the woods or the mines or the fisheries.[29] Other members of the farm household also contributed to family sustenance. Sons worked as agricultural labourers on farms that were productive enough to pay farm workers. Wives from poorer farms wove cloth and spun yarn for the families on wealthier farms. Daughters worked as domestic servants in the homes of the well-to-do farmers and merchants in the community. In most instances, this paid work was short-term, for all these family members also had work to do in their own households.[30] In short, what historians found in the rural communities of the Maritimes in the mid- and late nineteenth century was the family economy – that pattern of pre-industrial work in which every able-bodied member of the household, wives and daughters included, contributed labour to sustain life.[31]

Women's work in these rural families was broadly defined, but there was nonetheless a sexual division of labour, particularly in the realm of wage work. On the farm, wives and daughters might join husbands and sons in the fields, especially with haying and at harvest time. In September 1815, for example, Louisa Collins of Cole Harbour, Nova Scotia, wrote in her diary, "Mama and me went and pick'd sum pease and beans" and the next day, "I have bin makin hay till quite dark."[32] One hundred years later, Katie Margaret Gillis of Mabou Coal Mines, Cape Breton, was doing "the mowing when I was only 10 and 11 years old ... mowing and raking was my work."[33] However, there were also chores that fell exclusively to women, work done in, or close to, the home. Child care, care of dependent adults, food preparation, the home production of clothing and food (such as butter and cheese), the tending of gardens and livestock all were tasks left to wives and daughters. The paid labour that was available to girls and women also reflected this gendered division of family work: wives and daughters could sell any surplus butter and eggs, spin yarn, weave cloth, and sew clothing for wealthier families, and daughters could work in their households as domestic servants.[34]

SINGLE MARITIME WOMEN AND THE HISTORIOGRAPHY OF FEMALE MIGRATION

Two features of these studies of Maritime farm communities – the importance of daughters' paid and unpaid work to the subsistence of rural families and the experiences of some daughters as domestic

Young girls raking in the fields, Prince Edward Island, 1911 (Courtesy of the Public Archives and Records Office of Prince Edward Island, 2667/131)

servants – suggest a possible connection between the lives and responsibilities of these daughters and the upsurge of female out-migration in the second half of the nineteenth century. If the women who left the Maritimes were from rural areas, perhaps their motives for working far from home related to the reasons other young women went into the homes of neighbours: to help support their families. Put another way, the emigration of single women from the region may have been an act of obligation to the family and its economic needs.

To establish this connection it is necessary first to look at what is known about these migrants and then, for comparison, to examine briefly what historians have written about their counterparts from other regions of the world. A good place to begin is with Patricia Thornton's statistical breakdown of out-migrants. Thornton observed, for example, that most emigrants from the Maritimes in the late nineteenth century were single, and that among migrants to nearby cities in both the Maritime provinces and New England, single women outnumbered single men.[35] Aggregate statistics from the United States census of 1880 support her findings, revealing that Massachusetts attracted more Maritime immigrants than any other state. Similarly, 1885 data from the Massachusetts census indicate that female

Maritime immigrants to that state most frequently ended up in urban areas in and around Boston.[36]

Available literature on out-migration also points to the type of occupation Maritime women found once they arrived in the urban areas of eastern Massachusetts. For example, in his study of Maritimers in Boston, Brookes pointed out that a majority of the women became domestic servants rather than factory hands or garment piece-workers. My research on single Maritime women in Portland, Maine, reveals the same employment pattern.[37] Even in Lynn, Massachusetts, the shoemaking centre of the United States in 1880 and one of the top five cities in Massachusetts to attract Maritime women, the most common occupation of female Maritimers was domestic service.[38]

In addition to these statistical data, a seventy-year-old document rediscovered by Alan Brookes offers some valuable impressionistic evidence about Boston's Maritime immigrants in the first decades of the twentieth century. Written by Albert Kennedy, a social worker in Boston's South End Settlement House, "The Provincials" is a typical example of Progressive-era social commentary. At times moralistic and condescending it is nonetheless a rare source of information on these immigrants and includes observations about single women. According to Kennedy, such women were numerous, came from rural backgrounds ("daughters of the farmer-fisher folk of the Maritime Provinces"), and were of the "lower middle class." Kennedy also made an observation about Maritime women's occupations, noting that they were heavily represented not only in domestic service but also in other types of service such as hotel and restaurant work and in clerical work, nursing, and teaching.[39]

These statistics and observations are intriguing, for they suggest some commonalities among female emigrants from the Maritimes across the period of greatest out-migration: their rural origins, their preference for service and clerical work over factory labour, and their continued migration to nearby cities well into the twentieth century. Furthermore, these findings suggest that migrants shared a similar family background with the daughters of Maritimes farm households in the mid- and late nineteenth century whose labour in service helped support the family economy.

But more is missing than revealed in these scattered data and personal comments. They offer little insight into why young women left the Maritimes, or why they congregated in the Boston area and in service work. They leave other gaps in the historical record as well: where these women lived while in New England cities; what they did in their leisure time; what their relationships were to family and friends still in the Maritimes. At the same time these fragments point to a new and critical line of inquiry. Were the experiences and motivations of Maritime women in New England in the 1910s and 1920s different from those of their mothers' generation in the 1880s? If so, how do those differences modify our understanding of the whole process of Maritime out-migration?

One way to begin exploring these questions is by looking at research on other single women immigrants to North America in the nineteenth and early twentieth centuries. The body of historical work on immigrant women is substantial and touches on a wide range of issues affecting their lives, from reasons for leaving their home country, to family and kinship relationships, work experiences, community life, and social activism in their new homes. An annotated bibliography published in 1985 and several subsequent bibliographic essays attest to the richness of this historiography.[40] However, of all the literature covered in these works only a small percentage specifically addresses the experiences of single women immigrants, perhaps because in the migrant stream to North America they were a distinct minority. As Maxine Seller noted about migration to the United States, "during the nineteenth and early twentieth centuries male immigrants outnumbered female immigrants by roughly three to two," and single women were just a portion of the female immigrant group.[41] Not until after the Second World War and the upsurge of immigrants from Latin America, Asia, and the Caribbean did women outnumber men in the migrant stream to America.[42]

Nevertheless, available research on single migrant women reveals some similar behaviour patterns among women from different ethnic backgrounds. Female immigrants from Sweden, Finland, Germany, and the British Isles were the most likely of all Europeans to come to North America while single, and, like Maritime women in late-nineteenth-century New England, they were also likely to enter domestic service.[43] Furthermore, these women were entering service in an era when native-born women were looking for other employment because they found the role of family servant degrading and confining.[44] In her article on the historiography of women immigrants, Suzanne Sinké argued that these women preferred domestic service for economic and cultural reasons: it was "one of the most well paid occupations available to women," and – again like their counterparts from the Maritimes – "many of these women immigrants expected to serve in someone's household for at least part of their lives."[45] Studies of Irish immigrant women point to other factors as a possible explanation for the popularity of domestic service for single women migrants. Carole Groneman, for example, noted that young Irish women could find immediate employment in American as servants "and were particularly faithful in sending remittances to their families."[46] Janet A. Nolan calculated that fully 54 per cent of female born in Ireland were in service, and noted that they "participated in the family economy by supporting themselves, saving for their own and their sisters' dowries, sending cash remittances back to Ireland to maintain the family farm, and financing the emigration of siblings."[47]

The suggestion of a relationship connecting single women migrants from Europe, domestic service, and financial support for families still in the home country sets their migration in the broader context of their responsibilities as daughters to parental families. Recent research into family survival strategies in rural Nova Scotia has demonstrated that a daughter's labour, both paid and unpaid, represented a valuable component of the family economy. In North American cities, historians of working-class women have also noted that women's wage labour was inextricably connected to family responsibilities.[48] The economic needs of the family and the demands of household maintenance and child rearing dictated which female family members worked, at what age, and for how long. While boys were socialized to see work as a lifelong activity, girls were taught to expect to hold wage work only until they married, and if thereafter, only in times of desperate financial need. For example, in working-class families of Montreal, Bettina Bradbury observed, "males sought work for wages for most of their lives. For women such work was transitory, undertaken as girls, seldom as wives, but required if their husband died or deserted them."[49] According to Leslie Tentler, in early-twentieth-century America, sons in immigrant families worked, in part, as training to head a household in the future while daughters worked only to fulfil their responsibilities for family support. As a consequence, daughters were expected to hand over their pay envelopes to their mothers while sons often paid only room and board and could save or spend any leftover wages.[50]

This working-class belief that a daughter's primary duty as a wage earner was to support her family fits neatly into the patterns of the family economy in the rural Maritimes and reinforces the idea that a daughter's sense of duty to send money to the family followed her to New England. If Maritime families shared this belief, did it influence a migrant daughter's employment considerations and attitudes towards leaving home? Were her options for destination and work different from those of her brothers?

The limitation of most research on women, work, and the family economy is that the family unit under study was still intact. It is not clear that one can generalize from the behaviour of daughters living with their parents to those who left home, even country, to find work. Moreover, these studies do not address the question of whether migration was an expansion of the rural family economy or a liberation from family responsibilities. Aside from the example of Irish women who sent money back to their parents in Ireland, little in the current body of transatlantic migration literature offers any answers.

A study written in the late nineteenth century suggests a reason why the current literature is not helpful and also offers more fruitful line of inquiry for understanding female migration. In 1889 geographer E.G. Ravenstein published a paper based on patterns of migration in twenty European counties and entitled "The Laws of Migration." Among his "laws" were two that applied to women: first, that "females are more migratory than males" and, second, that "females appear to predominate among short-journey migrants."[51] The data from which he derived these laws were internal – that is, from within one country – and rural-to-urban. Taken together with the nature of his research base, the laws suggest that in the latter part of the nineteenth century short-distance migration from countryside to city in Europe was female-led, just as it was in the Maritime provinces. Later studies have largely confirmed Ravenstein's hypotheses.[52] Thus, literature on European women's work and migration may be useful for understanding the experiences of single women migrants from the Maritimes to nearby New England cities.

Within the large body of research on women and work in Europe, there are several studies that specifically link female rural-to-urban migration to job opportunities in cities and especially to the availability of positions in domestic service. The first historian to observe that the demand for servants in European cities attracted young women from poor rural families was Abel Chatelain, in his "Migrations et domesticité feminine urbaine en France, xviii–xxe siècles."[53] In a later study of women's work in Europe, Theresa McBride expanded on Chatelain's argument. In "The Long Road Home," she pointed out that domestic service was the largest source of paid work in the nineteenth century, employing "more women than all types of manufacturing put together," and that "domestic service in the industrial age frequently involved long-distance migration in search of positions in the cities."[54] McBride also suggested some reasons for the popularity of service for a rural European woman: better wages because room and board were provided, the opportunity to accumulate savings for marriage dowries, and the ability to send money home to her own family. In McBride's words, "Many a servant sent all or part of her wages to her parents, suggesting that many young women continued to think of the family as an economic unit."[55] Thus, in nineteenth-century Europe, there was an apparent connection between women's migration to work in cities and the preservation of the rural family economy.

A selective review of literature on women's work and rural-to-urban migration in the nineteenth and early twentieth centuries suggests several hypotheses about single women emigrants from the Maritimes living in New England. First, the majority probably came from rural areas and from families who were accustomed to having all able-bodied members contribute their labour to the collective goal of economic subsistence. Second, most women who left home travelled to the closest urban centres in New England, especially the Boston area, to find paid work – in the nineteenth century primarily as domestic servants, and later, in both service and clerical jobs. Finally, at least among those who were domestics, their motives for leaving home were neither to seek adventure nor to find skilled work, but to earn wages sufficient for them to send some money back to families in the Maritimes. Part 1 of this study will examine the validity of these suppositions.

However, testing hypotheses about the backgrounds and motives of Maritime female migrants to New England is just a first step in understanding the complex phenomenon of female emigration and work. Other questions remain. Why, for example, did out-migration of women from the Maritime provinces become so pronounced in the late nineteenth and early twentieth centuries? After all, according to existing research on Maritime emigration, sons, not daughters, were the shipbuilders and carpenters who sought employment where these skills were still in demand after such jobs had declined in the Maritimes. Also, Albert Kennedy noted that "Provincial" women in early-twentieth-century Boston were nurses, teachers, and shop clerks as well as domestics. This observation suggests that the types of jobs available to women had expanded by the 1910s and 1920s. Had young women's attitudes changed as well? Were the women who left the Maritimes in the early twentieth century more likely to seek less confining employment than domestic service? If so, what would that finding suggest about their life choices in relation to the needs of their families at home?

These questions both broaden the scope of the inquiry and raise the issue of changes over time in attitudes towards, and choice of, occupation for single women migrants. What is needed is a more comprehensive explanation that places the phenomenon of female out-migration from the Maritimes into the broader socio-economic context in which it occurred. Such an explanation must not only describe patterns of behaviour and family relationships but also explain changes in these patterns across the years between 1870 and 1930. That period in North America witnessed both the consolidation of capitalist enterprises into larger, more complex bureaucratic entities and an increase in consumer demand generated by new advertising and other marketing techniques. Historians such as Alice Kessler-Harris, in *Out to Work*, Elyce Rotella, in *From Home to Office*, and Veronica Strong-Boag, in *The New Day Recalled*, discuss the influence of changing economic structures on women's wage labour.[56] However, the most comprehensive analysis of the impact of industrial development on women's work – research that also addresses issues of female migration to cities – has come out of the literature on the European family and its adjustments to the changing demands of capitalist development.

In 1975 Joan Scott and Louise Tilly published an article that fellow scholar Michael Anderson described as "a seminal work pioneering the modern use of the concept of family."[57] Entitled "Women's Work and the Family in Nineteenth-Century Europe," the article explained the predominance of young, single women among female workers in terms of strategies that pre-industrial lower-class families, both peasant and artisan, developed to adjust to the changing economic structures of industrial capitalism.[58]

Scott and Tilly began their study by examining the economic function of the pre-industrial European family in terms similar to those of the nineteenth-century rural household in the Maritimes – the strategies of the family economy. Family-based production meant not only growing crops or carrying on a trade but also making clothes and processing food, work usually done by women. By the nineteenth century, however, the rise of factories gradually removed production from the home, and these families became increasingly dependent on cash to purchase goods they had once manufactured themselves. Women's work was especially affected as first cloth making, then food processing, and finally the manufacture of clothing went from home to factory. Earlier scholars had commented on the disruptive impact of industrial development on the family economy, but Scott and Tilly argued that the lower-class family's response was less disruption than adaptation of traditional patterns of behaviour to new situations.[59] Adaptation usually meant placing those members of the family least critical to the family production unit – often daughters – into the paid labour force. Scott and Tilly suggested that if the family were rural and jobs most available in cities, then these young women looked for urban work that best preserved old patriarchal family values such as deference to parents and protection of female virtue. Their study contended that the preponderance of rural young women in urban domestic service reflected, in part, the family's attempt to preserve pre-industrial values while adjusting to changing economic needs.[60]

Scott and Tilly described the adaptive behaviour of these families and rejected the notion that change in the mode of production led to immediate change in pre-industrial attitudes. At the same time their interpretation of familial response to industrial development contradicted a theory proposed by sociologist William J. Goode that changing ideology in the nineteenth century opened opportunities for women to leave home and earn wages. Goode argued that "Western women's high level of participation in the workplace was a result of the gradual, philosophical extension to women of Protestant notions about the rights and responsibilities of the individual [that] undermined the traditional idea of 'women's proper place.'"[61] Instead of choosing between a purely economic and a purely ideological model of social change, Scott and Tilly presented a third, more nuanced model, one that "posits a continuity of traditional values and behavior in changing circumstances."[62] Changes in attitude and behaviour of the family and its members do occur, they argued, but over time and with less disruption to long-held values than either of the other models suggests. According to Scott and Tilly, "behavior is less the product new ideas than of the effects of old ideas operating in new or changing contexts."[63] Many lower-class daughters worked in the nineteenth century because they had always worked; only the place of work changed, because families increasingly needed their wages more than they needed an extra pair of hands at home.

In their book *Women, Work, and Family,* Scott and Tilly refined their ideas about the European family response to industrialization and extended their analysis into the twentieth century.[64] They examined women's work across the past 250 years in terms of a three-stage model of family adjustment to economic change. The first stage was the pre-industrial "family economy," when women worked at home as part of the production unit. In the second stage, the "family wage economy," the family responded to structural changes wrought by the rise of industrial capitalism – the transformation of manufacturing from home to factory, the growth of a cash economy, the decline of small, family-owned units of production in the face of competition from larger, more heavily capitalized ones – by placing members no longer needed for home production into the paid workforce. Because the timing of industrialization varied in different European countries, the period of the family wage economy varied, encompassing most of the nineteenth century. The third stage of family adjustment began roughly with the beginning of the twentieth century and is labelled the "family consumer economy." It was during this stage that Tilly and Scott noted the rise of individualism in competition with concern for family needs.

The period of the family consumer economy coincided with the advanced stages of industrial capitalism, an era of business consolidation and rising consumer demand. Scott and Tilly observed several ways in which these changes influenced female family members. First, the growing size of business organizations and retail sales operations led to a changing job structure for women. Jobs in both domestic service and manufacturing declined while clerical and sales jobs, along with service and professional positions in teaching, nursing, and social service, increased. Working-class daughters entered all these fields, according to Scott and Tilly; thus, although they may still have worked to support the family, they were able to exercise more individual choices over what jobs they took and wages they earned. Scott and Tilly also argued that rising income levels among working-class families meant increasing standards of consumption both for the family as a whole and for its individual members. In return for their financial support, daughters began asking parents for money for leisure activities and for clothes. They also stayed in school longer and developed separate interests, friends, and sometimes values from those of their family. However, this sense of individualism developed slowly and took place in the context of a strong, on-going sense of family responsibility. New behaviours derived from new conditions were counterbalanced and modified by the persistence of traditional values.

Since its publication, *Women, Work, and Family* has been the target of some criticism and a contentious historiographic debate. Several scholars have noted, for example, that Tilly and Scott generalized to all of Europe from research focused primarily on England and France. In doing so, they not only made some unsupported assumptions about patterns of capitalist development in other countries but also discounted the role of distinct cultures in influencing family behaviour.[65] These criticisms are important caveats to consider when transferring this model to a North American setting. Different densities of population, different geographical and economic conditions, and different options, such as western migration, probably influenced North American family strategies for survival, and these factors need to be explored. Nevertheless the obvious parallels between what is known about female emigrants from the Maritimes and behaviour of European daughters in both the family wage and family consumer economies of Scott and Tilly's model point to the usefulness of that framework for examining the lives and experiences of these women.

However, Tilly and Scott's work has generated a more fundamental debate as well, one that focuses on the very concept of the family economy. Soon after *Women, Work, and Family* appeared, scholars began to question the assumption that the family was a cooperative institution with each member willingly contributing to its interests. In a 1981 article on housework, Heidi Hartmann argued that the working-class family did not share a "unity of interests" but rather was a "locus of struggle" rooted in the gender and class inequalities of a patriarchal and capitalist society.[66] In a study of the division of labour in the farm families of nineteenth-century Ontario, Marjorie Griffin Cohen placed this debate into a historical setting, arguing that within the pre-industrial rural family production unit, there was a division of power as well as labour. Among the farm families of Ontario (or Upper Canada) in the early nineteenth century, women were responsible for the subsistence activities of the farm – the care of farm animals, the maintenance of the family vegetable garden, the preparation of food, and so on – leaving husbands free to raise crops, usually wheat, for the commercial market. Thus, the work of women enabled men to make and invest profits and, thereby, control economic growth in the family.[67] Cohen did not argue that wives or daughters resisted, or were bothered by, this unequal division of economic power; but by presenting the family economy in terms of gender inequality, she also suggested the possibility of conflict in what had been described as a cooperative process. And, once introduced, the idea of conflict within the family production unit opens up the possibility that daughters looked for jobs in cities not to support but to avoid family authority and financial obligation.

In a 1988 study of single women migrants to Chicago, entitled *Women Adrift*, Joanne J. Meyerowitz made that very argument. She argued that "families did not always function as smoothly" as the "ideal family economy." Daughters left home not only because of economic necessity of family disruption but "because they had ambition and because they felt restricted, stigmatized, abused, unwanted or unhappy at home. Their presence in the city demonstrates that the real family economy sometimes failed to match the ideal."[68] This thesis directly contradicts the argument that daughters left rural families and found wage work in cities in order to send cash back home, and Meyerowitz's study would seem to present a serious challenge to the Tilly–Scott model of emigration as a family adaptation to the changing structures of capitalist development.

However, there are two serious limitations to Meyerowitz's study that undermine the strength of her argument and mute her criticism of the image of single women migrants as dutiful daughters. First, she consciously left domestic servants out of her study. She thus removed from consideration 47 per cent of all working women in 1880 and 33 per cent in 1900[69] (and presumably, live-in servants represented an even larger percentage of single wage-earning women living apart from their families). In removing domestics she left out the very women most likely to have considered family desires in choice of employment – the social control of living in a domestic setting, and the reduced expenses that allowed greater savings to be sent home. Second, she examined the lives of women migrants from 1880 to 1930 without taking into consideration that the profound changes in urban life during these years might have led to changes in behaviour and attitudes across the period. She commented on the independence of these women migrants and on their ability to survive in Chicago without family support by forming subcultures around their lives and work. However, this isolation from the family may well have been more typical of the 1920s than the 1880s, or – in Tilly and Scott's terminology – more typical of the period of the family consumer economy than that of the family wage economy.[70] At least the possibility should be explored.

Therefore, while Meyerowitz's observations about the separate world of "women adrift" in Chicago are important to consider, particularly for female migrants in the early twentieth century, they do not necessarily negate the value of the Tilly–Scott model of a collective family response to the structural changes of capitalist development. Their interpretation of the relationship of female migration to such family strategies remains the most compelling approach for exploring the experiences of Maritime-born women in Boston, many of whom had come from rural households and a culture of shared labour to support the family.

RECONSTRUCTING THE LIVES OF SINGLE MARITIME WOMEN IN BOSTON

By casting a research net across a wide expanse of secondary material it is possible to establish the historical setting in which single women from the Maritime provinces migrated to work in the Boston area. It is also possible to generate questions about their lives and attitudes that would place their experiences into the larger socio-economic context of industrial capitalist development and, thereby, broaden the entire historical understanding of Maritimes out-migration. However, answering these questions presents some daunting challenges. Beyond the usual problems attendant to writing the history of rural and working-class people – the lack of existing written expressions like letters and diaries, the paucity of references to their lives in other sources like newspapers or public documents – it is peculiarly difficult to reconstruct the lives of single women. Only nominal censuses consistently listed single women by name; other sources such as city directories listed only those living by themselves or as heads of households. Furthermore, once married, these women assumed their husbands' surnames, and tracing them in subsequent sources becomes virtually impossible.

Researching Maritime-born women, even in statistical records, presents additional problems. They often shared the same names; in the 1910 census year, for example, there were fourteen Mary McDonalds and three Mary MacDonalds living just in Boston's Ward 11. A more fundamental problem appears in the 1900, 1910, and 1920 nominal censuses, when census takers no longer included province in the birth places of Canadian residents of the United States. Instead, they divided the Canadian-born into two groups, "English Canadian" and "French Canadian," thus not only mixing the Maritime-born with other Canadians but artificially separating French-speaking Maritimers from their Anglophone neighbours. Any statistical information gathered from twentieth-century census materials requires substantial supporting evidence from other sources to ensure that it applies specifically to Maritimers in Boston.

Moreover, census and other statistical sources cannot fully answer the kinds of questions that address issues of motive, opinion, or emotional response. Numbers can describe but cannot explain behaviour; for explanation one must search out some form of personal expression. Fortunately, a few Maritime-born women who migrated to the Boston area left brief records of their experiences, either in their own words – in letters, diaries, and personal recollections – or in the anecdotes remembered by relatives and descendants. Several collections of primary sources include such materials: *No Place Like Home: Diaries and Letters of Nova Scotia Women, 1771–1938*, edited by Margaret Conrad, Toni Laidlaw, and Donna Smyth; *Away: Maritimers in Massachusetts, Ontario, and Alberta*, oral interviews collected by Gary Burrill; and interviews published in *Cape Breton's Magazine*. In addition, a letter I sent to over thirty newspapers in the Maritime provinces requesting information about Maritime women migrants generated over fifty letters from families describing the experiences of their mothers, grandmothers, and aunts who made the trip to New England. Finally, a few of these migrant women offered their own reminiscences in the form of taped interviews and conversations.

These personal recollections, undergirded with statistical evidence gathered from census materials and other public records, are the building blocks for reconstructing the world of single women from the Maritime provinces who migrated to Boston in the late nineteenth and early twentieth centuries. This world, too long neglected by scholars of the Maritimes, deserves attention; the part these women played in the drama of the exodus needs to be added to the historical record. But their experiences have a larger historical importance as well. They left home in greatest numbers during a particular period, one that witnessed the social and economic changes wrought by industrial capitalist development. By examining their lives in the context of these socio-economic transformations, we can compare their experiences to those of other women who left rural areas to work in nearby cities during the same period.

An initial review of the literature on single women migrants has pointed to the relationship of their behaviour to decisions of families back home and to changes in family dynamics across the years. Louise Tilly and Joan Scott developed this theme most fully in *Women, Work, and Family,* so their model of family adaptation to changing economic conditions will serve as the structural framework for this study. Using their model will make it possible both to compare the experiences of Maritime women to other single women migrants and to examine the validity of Tilly and Scott's theses in a North American context. There are fundamental questions to address in this process. How did capitalist development in the Maritime provinces affect rural production? Did families in the Maritimes respond to these changes in ways similar to the family strategies Tilly and Scott found in France and England? How did capitalist development transform the city of Boston in the years between 1870 and 1930, and how did these changes, in turn, affect the lives of the Maritime women who worked there? Finally, what, if any, role did these women themselves play in defining the nature of Maritime out-migration and, by extension, the nature of the Maritime provinces' response to the structural changes of capitalist development?

To set this study firmly into a context of structural changes, it is divided into two parts loosely following Tilly's and Scott's periods of family wage economy and family consumer economy. Part 1, "The Vanguard," focuses on the experiences of single women emigrants from the Maritimes who went to work in Boston in the late nineteenth century and formed the first generation of daughters to leave the country in large numbers. Part 2, "Eldorado," explores the lives, work, and attitudes of single Maritime women in Boston in the first three decades of the twentieth century, a second generation of female emigrants. The era of greatest exodus from the region began in the years following Confederation, so Part 1 opens with an exploration of economic conditions in the Maritimes in the 1860s through the 1880s. The relationship of these conditions to the departure of the first generation of single women to travel to New England's largest city, is the focus of the first chapter.

Finally, a note on the use of the term "generation." Historians often consider a generation to be about a twenty-year period.[71] In this study, however, the term is used more loosely. There are obviously more than twenty years separating the earliest and latest years of out-migration, and the process was continual, not episodic, across the period. Nevertheless, the concept of a generational divide is an important component in this analysis. It highlights another factor that may have influenced a young woman's decision to leave home: the rôle that the experiences of nineteenth-century single women emigrants may have played in altering family and community attitudes towards the cityward migration of young women in the early twentieth century.

PART ONE

The Vanguard

1 Changes at Home: The Maritime Economy and the Exodus, 1850–1890

Clara Peck was sixteen in 1878, the year she left her home in Nova Scotia, boarded a small coasting vessel, and sailed to Boston to find a job. One year later, her eighteen-year-old sister Alice followed Clara to the city to live and work.

Alice and Clara Peck were the eldest of six children. Until their departure they had lived with their widowed father Joshua, two brothers, and two sisters on a farm near Bear River, a small community fifteen miles inland from the port of Digby. According to the 1871 Nova Scotia census, Joshua Peck owned 600 acres – a large parcel of land for the region. However, the Peck farm itself was small: in 1871 only 37 of those acres were under cultivation. Cash was scarce, and Joshua apparently augmented his farm income by cutting timber on his land: when asked his occupation by the census taker, he listed both farmer and lumberman. The family often needed money for equipment and fertilizer, items that may once have been produced on the farm itself but in the 1870s were manufactured in factories far from Bear River. By 1878 their purchase required a larger cash outlay than the Pecks could afford to deduct from their meagre profits. Clara and Alice did not work in the fields, so their father looked to them for help in supplementing the family income. As the second daughter, Clara was free of Alice's responsibilities for younger siblings and was the first to look for wage-paying employment to help support the family. By the following year the other children were old enough to manage on their own, so Alice joined her sister.

Clara and Alice both chose to work in Boston rather than Halifax or Saint John. The 1870s were years of depression in North America, but New England had weathered the bad times more successfully than had the Maritime region, and jobs were both more plentiful and more lucrative in the prosperous cities of New England. Clara arrived in Boston and soon found a position as a domestic servant. When the head of the family for whom Clara worked decided to open a restaurant, Clara sent for Alice, who came with a friend to live with the family and work in the kitchen of the new establishment.

For the next twenty years, Clara continued to work as a domestic while Alice worked in the family's restaurant, Thompson's Spa, where she rose to the position of head pastry cook. During this time, both daughters faithfully sent a portion of their earnings back to their father in Nova Scotia to help with farm expenses. Working long hours, the women had little time for outside activities, so most of their social life centred around attendance at the Roxbury Adventist Church. Here Alice met John Edgar McKay, a ship's carpenter born in Nova Scotia, who worked in East Boston for the Lawley Shipbuilders. In 1901 the two were married.

The marriage proved short-lived; John McKay died only four years later, leaving Alice with a young son to support. She returned to work as a pastry cook, first in Bristol, Connecticut, and later in Northfield, Massachusetts, towns with Adventist churches, where she could find both spiritual and social support. Meanwhile, Clara remained single. She continued to work in Boston until their father was too old to manage alone, then moved back to Bear River to care for him. After Alice retired she, too, returned to Nova Scotia to spend the last years of her life on the farm where she had grown up.[1]

OUT-MIGRATION AND THE TRANSFORMATION OF THE MARITIME ECONOMY

Clara and Alice Peck were only two of thousands of men and women who left the Maritimes in the 1860s through the 1880s. Out-migration from the region was not a new phenomenon in 1860; in earlier decades some migrants, particularly immigrants from Ireland, had come to Maritime shores only to move to more rapidly developing parts of North America in search of settlement or work.[2] In fact, research suggests that this pattern of geographical and occupational mobility was the common experience of the nineteenth-century immigrant throughout North America.[3] However, in the 1870s out-migration took on a new and ominous cast. According to net migration estimates compiled by Patricia Thornton, for the first time the region began to lose more population than it gained from immigration. By the 1880s the differential was staggering: over 110,000 more persons were leaving the Maritimes than were moving in.[4] Only natural increase prevented the region from experiencing an absolute loss of population.

Newspapers in the Maritime provinces were quick to note the phenomenon. As early as 1869, the *New Brunswick Reporter and Fredericton Advertiser* commented on the out-migration of its "restless" youth.[5] In January 1870 the Halifax *Morning Chronicle* reported: "The Boston *Herald* of the 17th inst. publishes a statement of the 'Immigrants to Boston in 1869.' The total number of immigrants arrived in that city was 34,784, a larger number than in any single year previous ... They represent 36 nationalities ... Nova Scotia stands third on the list of countries [, supplying] 6,026, of which 3,361 were males and 2,665 were females."[6] In April 1873 the *Acadian Recorder* reported its own study of Nova Scotian migrants to the United States in the summer of 1872. According to its findings, 693 men and 831 women had arrived in that country, and 923 were between the ages of fifteen and forty. Also listed was a breakdown of occupations; among the emigrants were farmers, mariners, carpenters and assorted other craftsmen, merchants, professionals, servants, and seamstresses.[7]

A recurrent theme in these articles was the young age of those who were leaving the Maritimes. There was palpable concern not only that the region was losing population but that it was losing the next generation. This concern was well founded. Thornton's research into the demographics of the exodus reveals that "migration was heavily concentrated among the young active age groups who lost between 20 and 50 per cent of their numbers in any decade, or three to four times the rate from the population at large."[8] If young Maritimers were abandoning their native provinces, they were taking their skills, their energy, and their potential with them, and regional decline would surely follow. It was imperative to find the reason for their departure and to discourage them from leaving.

The newspapers blamed the exodus on everything from youthful restlessness, greed, and sloth to misguided notions of greener pastures on the other side of the region's borders. "We regret to notice," chided the Kings County, New Brunswick, *Record*, "the number of young men who are going to the States this Spring. If these young men would work as hard at home as they do in the States they could live more comfortably at home than they will ever be able to do away."[9] To stem the outflow, editors and correspondents would report with evident relish the sad fate of those who sought their fortunes elsewhere. For example, a correspondent for the Charlottetown *Daily Examiner* observed that "those who were foolish enough to leave the Maritime Provinces for the West, during the recent 'Colorado' or 'Kansas' craze, are beginning to return home even sooner than expected ... doubtless many who have gone from the Lower Provinces in haste are by this time repenting in leisure."[10] When the subject was young women, the theme of regret was sometimes embellished with lurid episodes of seduction and abandonment, as in the following report in the 8 December 1876 edition of the Halifax *Citizen*:

A HALIFAX GIRL'S WRETCHED FATE. Mr. Charles M. Levin about four weeks ago found a young girl in a wretched condition in one of the dens on Richmond Street. She was in a destitute condition, lying in an unoccupied room on a sofa. She was taken to City Hospital on the first of the month ... victimized by a married man after obtaining a situation as a table girl in one of the fashionable hotels.[11]

Ultimately, however, neither cautionary tales nor editorials had much effect on the decisions of Maritimers to emigrate, and in the last three decades of the nineteenth century over 300,000 of them left the region.[12] Scholars, seeking reasons for this exodus, have had little difficulty finding possible explanations. From the 1860s to the 1880s – years of the first upsurge of out-migration – the Maritime provinces experienced a series of political and economic jolts that combined to disrupt, and ultimately undermine, the traditional economy of the region.

In the middle of the nineteenth century the Maritimes consisted of three separate British colonies – Nova Scotia, New Brunswick, and Prince Edward Island – each with its own colonial government and historical peculiarities. Prince Edward Island had been established by the British government under a system of land tenure whereby absentee proprietors controlled large land grants and the settlers who improved the land could not easily gain title to it. Not until 1875 was the proprietor system fully replaced with freehold land tenure.[13] New Brunswick was unique in its primary export, wood products from the vast forests of its interior.[14] Among the three provinces Nova Scotia had the most diversified economy and was the only one with a coal mining industry.

Still, by comparison with other regions of North America, especially central Canada and the United States, the Maritime provinces had much in common. All three were largely rural and were sparsely settled, with small communities scattered mostly along their coastlines or river valleys.[15] Their economic life line was the Atlantic Ocean. They sailed their wooden ships east to Great Britain and south to the United States and the West Indies to sell timber, fish, coal, and agricultural products and buy sugar, flour, and manufactured goods.[16] In the larger towns, merchants owned the vessels that plied the ocean and handled the region's maritime trade; in the smaller communities much of the population traded their produce or their labour for cash or credit spent at merchants' stores. In the Maritime provinces at mid-century the structures of mercantile capitalism were well entrenched.[17]

But in the three decades that followed, these structures cracked and finally crumbled under the strain of political and economic changes that reoriented the Maritime economy away from the Atlantic and integrated it with the economy of central Canada. The first step in this process was the decline in the Maritimes' coastal and ocean trade when, in the 1840s, the British embraced the philosophy of free trade, abandoning its policy of preferential trade with its colonies. For a time, reciprocal trade agreements with the United States for staple goods compensated for the loss of timber and agricultural trade with the British, but following the disruptions of the American Civil War the United States abandoned its policy of reciprocity and levied tariffs on Maritime products.

The next step involved the political union of the Maritime provinces, the United Province of the Canadas, and British Columbia to form a single dominion that extended to the Pacific. In the Maritimes there was strong opposition to such a plan. To marshal support, advocates of Confederation offered an economic enticement: they promised that the new federal government would pay to finish construction of a railroad connecting the region with the major cities of central Canada. By 1873 (when a reluctant Prince Edward Island finally agreed to the terms of Confederation) all three Maritime provinces had become part of Canada; in 1876 the Intercolonial Railway was completed, with its headquarters in Moncton, New Brunswick, and its lines extending from Halifax to Rivière-du-Loup in Quebec.[18] In return for gaining rail connections to the rest of the country, the Maritimes became a small appendage of a vast transcontinental region with its political and economic centre at roughly its geographical centre – the provinces of Quebec and Ontario.

The final step in the process of integration of the Maritime economy with the rest of Canada was the implementation of the National Policy, a series of high protective tariffs on Canadian resources and manufactured goods. Created by the Conservative government in Ottawa, the tariffs were designed to encourage the development of Canadian industry by making imported goods prohibitively expensive for Canadian consumers – to establish intra-provincial east–west trade and undermine north–south trade with the United States. To adjust, the Maritime provinces would have to replace their sea-going mercantile economy with a land-based manufacturing economy able to compete with their larger, more industrialized neighbours in central Canada.

For a short time the benefits of the National Policy seemed real. In what one historian has described as the "hothouse industrial growth of the eighties, industrial development flourished in the Maritimes in the early 1880s, exceeding by 15 per cent even that of central Canada."[19] Iron and steel plants, sugar refineries, and rope factories were built, and, in the most dramatic upsurge of industrial development of the period, seven cotton textile mills were constructed in New Brunswick and Nova Scotia just between 1882 and 1885.[20] According to the principles of the National Policy, the growth of these and other enterprises would compensate for the decline in the staples trade of wood, fish, and agricultural produce. Merchants would invest their profits in manufacturing while surplus labour from the farms and woods would become the workforce to run the new factories. In this fashion, regional industrial capitalism would replace the old merchant capitalist economy of the Maritimes.

But it did not happen quite that way. According to historian T.W. Acheson, some Maritime businessmen, more comfortable operating in a commercial economy, were unwilling to invest the necessary capital to build a strong industrial base.[21] At the same time overproduction and economic depressions in the 1870s and mid-1880s weakened those manufacturing enterprises that did exist, making such investments even more risky. Exacerbating all these difficulties was the threat of competition from larger, more heavily capitalized producers in Quebec and Ontario. The Intercolonial Railway, built to carry Maritimes products to central Canada, also carried goods in the other direction, swamping the region with cheaper manufactures from the West. The larger businesses of central Canada could weather bad economic times more easily than the struggling enterprises of the Maritimes, many of which failed or fell victim to purchase by outside interests. At the same time, the traditional carrying trade in locally made and owned wooden sailing vessels continued its inexorable decline, replaced by transportation on rail and in iron-clad steamships. Even some local financial institutions collapsed, most notably the Bank of Prince Edward Island.[22] By the end of the nineteenth century it was painfully obvious to many Maritimers that industrial capitalism had largely replaced their mercantile economy, but it was a Canada-wide industrial capitalism, dominated by financiers from central Canada for their own benefit and beyond the control of the region.

The coincidence of regional economic decline in the 1880s and 1890s and the dramatic rise in emigration from the Maritimes has led historians of out-migration to conclude that the two phenomena were inextricably connected. There is substantial evidence to support this idea. As Alan Brookes has demonstrated in his research on Maritimers living in Boston, a high percentage of the men working there were fishermen, carpenters, wooden shipbuilders, and other skilled craftsmen thrown out of work when the traditional staples trade and shipbuilding industries declined.[23] Brookes also examined out-migration from one community in Nova Scotia – Canning – that had been tied to the traditional mercantile and shipbuilding economy and was left off the rail line from Annapolis to Windsor that connected to the Intercolonial Railway. The impact of economic deterioration on out-migration in Canning was apparent; by 1892, "one in four of Canning's population had joined the Exodus."[24] As a dissenting voice, Patricia Thornton has argued that young Maritimers, attracted by better jobs and wages in other parts of North America, left home before the region suffered its worst economic dislocations and that their absence contributed to the failure of the region to industrialize.[25] In fact, both Brookes and Thornton may be right; the relationship between economic decline and emigration may have been an interactive process, with each factor having a multiplier effect on the other.

Nevertheless, something is still missing in both these interpretations. Although shipbuilders, fishermen, and carpenters might choose, or be driven, to leave the Maritimes because the region failed to replace its mercantile economy with a lasting industrial base, it is less clear how the economic travails of the region impelled the Peck sisters to go to Boston to become domestic servants and restaurant workers. And, in the 1870s and 1880s, women like Alice and Clara Peck represented a majority of those who left.[26] In the words of historian Margaret Conrad, they "marched in the vanguard of the exodus."[27]

ECONOMIC CHANGE, THE FAMILY ECONOMY, AND FEMALE OUT-MIGRATION

Out-migration of young women from the Maritime provinces took place in the same years and in the same historical context as that of the young men in the region. The momentous changes of the period doubtless had an impact on the lives of daughters as well as sons and influenced their decisions to leave. However, the role that economic transformation played in female out-migration needs to be explored separately because in nineteenth-century North America life choices of women were circumscribed in ways that did not apply to men. Young men, carrying the responsibility for supporting the next generation, were encouraged to find work that best suited their individual skills, interests, and ambition. Economic need might limit, even determine, their choices, but personal success could always remain a goal, if only as a distant dream. Young women, on the other hand, were expected to place responsibility to their family – first that of their parents and, after marriage, that of their husband – above personal goals. Individual ambition, personal financial gain, and career aspirations were discouraged among women throughout much of the century, as barriers to higher education and most professions made abundantly clear.[28] In the context of these societal expectations, most young women, like the Peck sisters, were unlikely to break a well-established precedent and leave the Maritimes purely for their own interests.

Instead, as responsible daughters, Clara and Alice Peck went to work as a domestic servant and a kitchen worker specifically to earn money to help with the family farm expenses, something daughters in rural Maritime households had been doing for decades. Unlike young women from earlier generations, however, they travelled great distances to find work and remained there for long stretches of time. What had changed in the years between their mother's youth and their own that allowed, or forced, them to look for work in distant cities rather than local neighbourhoods? And what, if any, role did economic conditions in the region play in bringing about this change? To answer these questions it is necessary first to examine the family lives of rural Maritime women in the years before the exodus, because it was in this world that the first generation of female emigrants were raised.

Clara and Alice Peck were born in the early 1860s, the closing years of what Maritimers have often labelled the region's "Golden Age," before Confederation and economic integration with Canada spelled the end of the Maritimes' mercantile or "wood, wind, and sail" economy. Major components of the Golden Age myth were the optimism of the region's citizenry and the roughly egalitarian nature of its rural society. At mid-century the majority of household heads in the region were farmers, and according to the collective memory of later generations they were, in the main, self-sufficient producers. According to one description, they were "happy and honest, independent and industrious, turning their hands to a range of tasks, sheltered from the ills of the world, and providing for their own and succeeding generations ... veritable yeoman."[29]

However, recent historical research into rural communities of the Maritimes has unearthed a quite different reality. Far from being egalitarian, rural society at mid-century was sharply stratified. A few farm and merchant families were at the top and had surplus capital to invest or spend on hired labour, but the subsistence of a majority of farm families was tenuous enough to require outside wages.[30] Out of this reality came the tradition of "occupational pluralism" that characterized the working life of many Maritime heads of households, including farmer/lumberman Joshua Peck. From this reality also emerged the strategy of the family economy that consigned all able-bodied household members to contribute their labour, paid and unpaid, to family production.[31]

For daughters, contribution to the family economy often included time spent working for wages in the households of nearby families. But these women seldom could spent long periods of time away from home because they were also needed by their own family to help with the many tasks of household production relegated to women. Among the most demanding of these were the preparation of clothing and food for the family. Clothing production involved carding wool, spinning yarn and thread, weaving cloth, and then cutting, piecing together, and sewing each article of apparel, all without any mechanical aids beyond a spinning wheel. And food preparation went far beyond providing daily meals to include caring for livestock, gathering eggs, milking cows, churning butter, gathering and preserving fruits and vegetables, salting fish and meats, and storing root crops to prevent spoilage. Given this critical need for female household labour, what happened in the succeeding years that enabled Joshua Peck, a widowed farmer with six children, to allow his two eldest daughters to emigrate to Boston to find work?

One answer lies in the impact of industrial capitalist development on the family production unit. The same forces of economic transformation that undermined the mercantile economy of the Maritimes also altered the nature of the family economy, especially home production. Although no full study has yet been done on the effect of these changes on the rural Maritime family, research on other parts of North America reveals that tasks traditionally done at home – especially carding, spinning, and weaving – were among the first replaced by factory production.[32] Evidence from agricultural censuses of the region suggests that such changes were taking place in all three Maritime provinces. Between 1871 and 1891 domestic (family-based) cloth production in the Maritimes declined steadily; in the second decade alone the quantity of hand-woven cloth dropped from 2,802,553 to 1,622,856 yards (see table A.1 in appendix A). In the same two decades, the number of woollen mills in New Brunswick and Nova Scotia increased from fourteen to twenty-four (plus seven in Prince Edward Island, which was not included in the 1871 count), and the number of cotton mills in the Maritimes grew from two to seven.[33] By the 1880s butter and cheese were also being produced in factories.[34] As household production declined, so did the economic contribution of home-bound daughters.

Women were not the only members of Maritime households to feel the repercussions of industrial capitalist development. With the completion of the Intercolonial Railway and the enactment of high tariffs on foreign goods, capitalists of central Canada realized their dream of an integrated Canadian economy; the impact of these changes on the individual family producer was considerable. The regional industrial development of the period led to the growth of cities and towns and to increased demand for produce from surrounding farms. The transformation from home to factory production extended to farm implements and consumer goods, which flowed into the region in ever greater numbers. At the same time, railroads that carried factory goods also brought agricultural products, and Maritime farmers found themselves in competition with larger, more heavily capitalized farms in central and western Canada. The response of individual Maritime farmers was to expand their operations and gear their production more to the demands of external markets. One indication of this approach was the increase in the total area of land improved for agriculture throughout the second half of the nineteenth century, from 1,443,000 acres in 1851 to 4,222,000 acres in 1891.[35] On that land, farmers raised more commercial crops, such as apples and dairy products, and less grain, which could be grown more profitably in Ontario and on the Prairies (see tables A.2, A.3, and A.4 in appendix A).

Expanded operations, specialized production, and increased dependence on factory-produced goods all meant a growing need for cash – to buy land, implements, and household items. The conjunction in these years of a rising demand for cash and the decline of household production suggests that daughters could be of more economic benefit to their families by earning wages than by remaining at home. But the number of employment opportunities in local villages was limited. The only available wage work besides domestic service was teaching in the local one-room school, an option restricted to better-educated young women – and, in some regions

A school teacher and her students, Kings County, Nova Scotia, c. 1896
(Courtesy of the Nova Scotia Archives and Records Management, N-1189)

like Cape Breton Island, still a male-dominated profession.[36] Since daughters could now be farther from home without jeopardizing family production, a logical solution was for these young single women to go to nearby cities to find work. The likelihood that this migration took place is borne out by census data; by 1871, in both Nova Scotia and New Brunswick, single men outnumbered single women in rural areas while single women outnumbered single men in urban areas (see table 1).

FEMALE OUT-MIGRATION IN THE 1870s AND 1880s: DESTINATIONS

Statistics on net migration from New Brunswick, Nova Scotia, and Prince Edward Island compiled by Patricia Thornton reveal that by the 1870s a sizeable percentage of young women were also willing – or were compelled by lack of job opportunities – to travel beyond provincial borders to seek employment. In fact, when Thornton's figures are averaged across the three Maritime provinces, the net migration loss of women from the region exceeded that of men for the last three decades of the nineteenth century. In the 1870s 50.5 out of every 1,000 women emigrated, as compared to 38.9 out of every 1,000 men. In the 1880s the emigration rates had risen to 139.3 per 1,000 women and 127.9 per 1,000 men; in the 1890s the rates were 134.7 per 1,000 women and 122.7 per 1,000 men.[37]

Table 1
Single men and women in New Brunswick and Nova Scotia
living in rural and urban areas,* 1871

	Single men	Single women	Sex ratio: males per 100 females
Rural areas	235,372	228,404	103
Urban areas	11,783	13,009	91

Source: Census of Canada, 1870–71 (Ottawa: I.B. Taylor, 1873).

* Urban areas include the three largest cities in each province: Saint John (pop. 28,805), Portland (12,520), and Fredericton (6,006) in New Brunswick; Halifax (29,582), Yarmouth (5,335), and Dartmouth (4,358) in Nova Scotia. Rural areas include the rest of the provinces.

It is impossible to know the exact destination of all those who left the region in these years, but both descriptive and statistical evidence can shed some light on the issue. For example, newspaper articles on the exodus often referred to "harvest excursions," seasonal trips to the Canadian Prairies to work as farm labour during the harvest season. In August 1899 the *Acadian Recorder* announced:

The Canadian Pacific Railway Co, have been advised by their agents in the west that something over 5,000 laborers will be required in Manitoba and Assiniboia to assist in harvesting the great wheat crop of 1899, and in order to provide assistance for the farmers there, arrangements have been made to sell second-class farm laborers' excursion tickets from all coupon ticket stations in the Maritime Provinces.[38]

Two weeks later the Amherst *Daily News* painted a less encouraging picture of opportunities for work on Prairie farms with the headline "HUNGRY MEN IN MANITOBA. Demand work or food and say they have been defrauded."[39] The harvest excursions were evidently attempts by large agricultural interests to create a surplus of farm workers and thereby keep wages at a minimum. They were also male preserves.

Other long-distance opportunities (some genuine, some bogus) beckoned the young men of the Maritimes to go west. The *Trades Journal* of the Provincial Workmen's Association, a union of Nova Scotia miners, often reported job opportunities outside the region – for example, in Pennsylvania, central Colorado, and New Mexico.[40] In September 1881 an advertisement in the Halifax *Morning Herald* proclaimed, "men wanted" in Winnipeg for "bricklayers ... hod-carriers, carpenters, labourers."[41] Sometimes the newspapers spoke of more permanent options for settlement. As early as 1870 the

Halifax *Morning Chronicle* posted an advertisement for "splendid inducements to emigrants," including "good wages, constant employment, and a farm of 80 acres of magnificent land for nothing, on the line of an important railway" in Minnesota.[42]

A similar notice in the *Nova Scotian* in 1884 appealed directly to the advantages of farming in the American Midwest and the difficulties of agriculture in the Maritimes:

DAKOTA–MINNESOTA

The Chicago Northwestern Railway now has for sale nearly 1,000,000 acres of the choicest FARMING LANDS ... 2$ to 6$ per acre ... leave the marshes, stumps, stones and worn-out lands of the East.[43]

While the West provided enticements for young men to leave farms and struggling communities and seek farm labour, mine work, skilled and semi-skilled jobs, or homesteading opportunities, there seem to have been no comparable attractions for female Maritimers.

Instead, if contemporary news items are to be believed, young women set out for the cities of New England. Newspaper references to female emigrants often took the form of reports from other newspapers or private sources about conditions in Boston for young women who were considering going there. The stories were uniformly bleak cautionary tales. The Kings County, New Brunswick, *Record* of 25 October 1889, for example, excerpted a long article from the Boston *Herald* on "Sewing Girls of Boston," stating:

Thousands of women come from "Down East" and the provinces to seek occupation. They abandon the quiet of their village homes for the great heartless city, believing that life here has no shadows. Many of them find, to their everlasting sorrow, that it is all shadows. After once getting here, they dislike to go back, and accept pauperizing wages rather than return to their friends.[44]

A news story appearing some ten years later in the Amherst *Daily News* claimed to quote from a "letter in private hands recently received from Boston" that "an influx of young girls from the blue-nose land was so large that wages of those who go to live out at service are largely reduced."[45] The moral of these reports for young women was clear: don't go to Boston to look for work; there are already so many of your sisters there that you will be disappointed in your search.

Whether or not there was any substance to these accounts, they were all based on a common idea: that young women leaving the Maritime provinces were heading in great numbers to the Boston

Table 2
Massachusetts cities with the greatest number of Maritime-born residents, 1885

City	Males	Females	Sex ratio: males per 100 females
Boston	9,243	14,481	64
Gloucester	2,022	1,556	130
Cambridge	1,424	1,879	76
Lynn	930	1,365	68
Chelsea	1,138	1,878	76

Source: Carroll D. Wright, The Census of Massachusetts, 1885 (Boston: Wright and Potter, 1887–88).

area. Statistics from United States and Massachusetts censuses substantiate this perception. In 1880 the state with the greatest number of residents born in New Brunswick, Nova Scotia, and Prince Edward Island was Massachusetts, with 44,926. The second highest total was in Maine, with 17,894 Maritime-born residents – less than 40 per cent of the number in Massachusetts, despite Maine's common border with New Brunswick and its proximity by land or sea to the other two Maritime provinces.[46] Furthermore, according to its 1885 census, the state of Massachusetts had 64,097 Maritime-born residents, of which 37,412 were women and 26,685 were men. Thus, females Maritimers outnumbered their male counterparts in the most popular American destination for out-migrants from the region.[47]

The 1885 Massachusetts census also included statistics on the place of birth of the residents of its cities. Table 2 lists the five cities with the most Maritime-born residents in 1885, broken down by sex. Several aspects of these statistics are striking. First, in four of the top five cities women outnumbered men; only in Gloucester, a major fishing port, did men predominate. Second, four of the five cities (again, Gloucester being the exception) were within fifteen miles of each other, and three of the five – Boston, Chelsea, and Cambridge – were contiguous. The centre of this constellation of urban areas, and by far the most popular destination, was Boston. (See figure 1.)

Four of the five destination cities had another characteristic in common: they were not "factory towns." In the second half of the nineteenth century, the map of Massachusetts was dotted with communities, large and small, dominated by industries, often textile mills. From North Adams in western Massachusetts to Southbridge in the southern part of the state to Lowell and Lawrence in the northeast, the "mill town" was a common feature of the state and a frequent destination for immigrants seeking employment. In the early nineteenth century, the daughters of New England farmers had

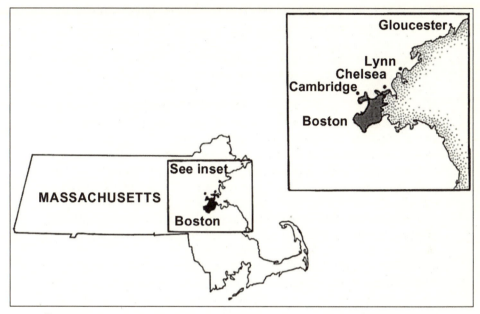

Figure 1
Map of Massachusetts showing location of cities with the greatest number of
Maritime-born residents, 1885

formed the first labour force in the cotton factories of Lowell, and as
late as 1860 a majority of mill operatives were still young, single
women. In 1870, the Lowell mills claimed 132 Maritime-born women
among its workers.[48] However, by the end of the American Civil War,
these women were a remnant in the textile mill workforce. Most
single women, dependent on subsistence wages for survival, were
replaced by poor immigrant families – first from Ireland, then French
Canada, and later from southern and eastern Europe – who were
willing to place several family members in the mill to compensate
for individual workers receiving less than a living wage.[49]

The one industrial city that continued to attract women migrants
throughout the nineteenth century was Lynn, the centre of the shoe
industry in Massachusetts and the acknowledged leader throughout
North America in the production of fine women's footwear. According to historian Mary Blewett, in 1880 "the female workforce in Lynn
were still overwhelmingly young, single, native-born New Englanders," and "even the foreign-born from Nova Scotia with Scottish and
English backgrounds shared basically similar cultural values with the
Yankees."[50] Why Lynn's shoe industry remained immune to the

impact of immigrant labour and wage competition for longer than other industries employing women is not clear. Whatever the reasons, in the post–Civil War period women could earn substantially higher wages in shoe factories than they could in textile mills. According to a study of women and work by Hull House researcher Edith Abbott, women shoe fitters and stitchers in the early 1870s earned from $7 to $14 a week.[51] By contrast, wages for female cotton textile operatives ranged from $3.50 to $8 a week.[52] Thus, a combination of high wages and a congenial workforce made up of young women from similar backgrounds apparently served to draw Maritime women to Lynn and its shoe factories even as they avoided other factory towns. At least one Maritime-born shoe worker in Lynn, Hannah Richardson, was able to save enough from her earnings to send money to her family in Yarmouth, Nova Scotia, suggesting that wages high enough to allow a young woman to help with family finances may have been another attraction of Lynn's shoe factories.[53]

But the example of Lynn remains an exception. The most popular destination for single Maritime-born women was Boston. It was the place they came to know and the source of the memories they brought back to family and friends. As the Maritimer's popular name for New England – the "Boston States" – reveals, that city became the emblematic destination for emigrants from the Maritimes, especially young women. It is clear that exploring the lives and experiences of single women migrants in Boston is fundamental to any understanding of female out-migration from the Maritimes.

Before beginning this exploration, it is worthwhile to review what has been established about the world that young Maritime women left and the reasons they left it. Two themes emerge that point to reasons for the sudden upsurge of female out-migration in the 1870s and 1880s. First, economic dislocations brought about by the integration of the region with the rest of Canada and the impact of industrial capitalist development played a critical role in impelling both young men and young women – the majority of emigrants – to leave the region. Second, the *way* that economic change influenced the decision to emigrate differed somewhat for sons and daughters. While some sons likely left home just for part-time work to help the family – on harvest excursions in Manitoba or on fishing vessels out of Gloucester, Massachusetts – others responded to declining economic opportunities by seeking better prospects for themselves, as farmers, miners, and carpenters, in places far from the Maritimes. By contrast, daughters headed to nearby cities to find paid work, and, as figures in chapter 2 will show, the majority ended up working as domestics in the households of other families – the same kind of work their mothers might have done as daughters to help support their families, only in local neighbourhoods rather than large metropolises. As home production was replaced by factory-made goods, a daughter's economic contribution to the household declined. Families apparently adjusted by sending daughters away to work in urban areas as a new means of financial support for the household. In following this practice, families in the Maritimes were responding to the impact of capitalist development in a way similar to that of their counterparts in much of industrializing Europe through the nineteenth century.[54]

To assign a single motive to the collective behaviour of several thousand women is to risk making a sweeping and indefensible generalization. Without a doubt, young women left home for many reasons, ranging from a desire for adventure and freedom from parental control to a desperate need to escape physical or sexual abuse. Nevertheless, the fact that economic dislocation in the Maritimes coincided with the first wave of female emigration from the region makes the idea of a shared motive of support for family at home seem plausible, and the experiences of Alice and Clara Peck bolster this hypothesis.

2 Single Maritime Women in Boston, 1880

According to verifiable entries in the US nominal census, there were 4,166 single women from the three Maritime provinces living in Boston in 1880.[1] Like Clara and Annie Peck, the great majority of these women were young – over 70 per cent were under thirty years old (see table 3). Most – 3,713, or nearly 90 per cent – were also employed. Nearly half of the single Maritime-born girls and women living in Boston in 1880 had arrived within the last ten years; the 1870 census for the city listed only 2,384 such women. Thus, the 1870s, the decade of such pivotal economic changes in the Maritimes, also witnessed a substantial rise in migration of single women from New Brunswick, Nova Scotia, and Prince Edward Island to find work in Boston.[2]

BOSTON IN 1880

To travel from the Maritimes to Boston was to leave a world of rural villages and small cities and enter an urban metropolis of 362,839 inhabitants.[3] In 1880 the city was in the midst of fundamental changes that would transform it from a New England mercantile city to an industrial, intellectual, and commercial centre. One of the most profound changes was in the composition of its residents. A relatively homogeneous group of New Englanders, British immigrants, and a few Germans in 1845, the Boston population was irrevocably altered between the 1850s and 1870s, when thousands of post-famine Irish Catholics arrived in the city. Desperately poor and subject to

Table 3
Age of single Maritime women in Boston, 1880

Age	Number	% of total
0–9 years	23	.6
10–19 years	634	15.2
20–9 years	2,326	55.8
30–9 years	770	18.5
40–9 years	260	6.2
50 and over (includes missing cases)	153	3.7
Total	4,166	100.0

Source: US Census of Population, 1880, Schedule no. 1: Boston, Suffolk County, Massachusetts, in US National Archives and Records Service, *Tenth Census of the United States, 1880* (Washington: NARS, 1960), reels 552–62.

virulent prejudice from the city's Protestant elites, these immigrants faced limited employment opportunities and became the proletariat on which the city built its industrial base. According to Oscar Handlin, in *Boston's Immigrants, 1780–1865*, the number of industrial workers in Boston quadrupled in the two decades immediately following the 1846 Potato Famine, and in 1865 Boston ranked fourth in the country as a manufacturing city.[4] Among the industrial enterprises built or expanded in the years after the arrival of the Irish were sugar refineries, clothing factories, iron works, shoe manufacturers, sewing machine factories, and piano and organ manufacturers.[5]

In 1875 there were some 60,000 Irish-born inhabitants of Boston.[6] Most lived in the crowded tenements and rundown houses of the older parts of the city, especially Wards 6, 7, and 8 – the old North and West Ends. (For location of districts and wards in Boston, see figure 2.) By 1880, however, some Irish-born Bostonians had saved enough money to rent or purchase housing further from the crowded city core – in Charlestown and especially in South Boston's Ward 13. At the same time in the teeming streets of the immigrant North End, one could sometimes hear the sounds of Italian and Portuguese mixing with the more familiar Irish brogue, as the first southern Europeans began arriving to add their numbers to the industrial labour force.[7]

It was not just the immigrant working class that swelled Boston's population in the three decades before 1880. These years also witnessed an enormous growth in the city's middle class, through repeated extension of the city limits to include surrounding residential areas. The primary means of city growth consisted of a series of annexations by Boston of surrounding towns. In the 1850s Boston

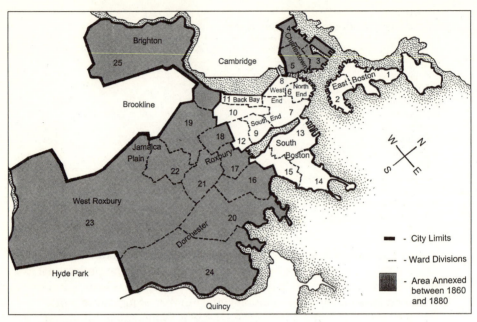

Figure 2
Boston, 1880, showing ward divisions and areas annexed 1860–80

took over parts of Roxbury and Dorchester, and in 1868 the whole town of Roxbury became a part of the city. In similar fashion, in the 1870s, Boston claimed first part of Brighton, then all of that community, as well as Dorchester, Charlestown, and West Roxbury. By such means the city dramatically increased both its area and population (see figure 2.)[8] The establishment and expansion of street railways from these outlying communities to the city centre led to a constant growth in numbers of single- and multiple-family homes in price ranges to fit virtually any middle-class budget.[9]

Pressed on all sides by the growing immigrant population, the elite of the city also sought newer quarters, close to their traditional enclave on Beacon Hill but buffered from the onslaught of the newcomers. After 1870, when the Back Bay behind the old city was filled in, this area – separated from the old North and West Ends by the Boston Common and Public Gardens – offered an ideal location, and the wealthy rushed to build elegant town houses along Beacon Street, Marlborough Street, and Commonwealth Avenue.[10] Their enthusiasm for constructing new and grand edifices did not end with housing but included intellectual and cultural institutions as well, such as the building that housed the Museum of Natural History and the

Massachusetts Institute of Technology (on Berkeley Street between Boylston and Newbury Streets), the original Harvard Medical School (on Boylston and Exeter Streets), and the proposed site for a new Boston Public Library in Copley Square. They also supported the construction of civic institutions such as the impressive three-building complex of the Boston City Hospital (in the city's South End) and a new city hall downtown.[11]

Thus, by the last quarter of the nineteenth century, the city of Boston had all the elements of a dynamic and rapidly growing major metropolis. Going to such a place must have seemed an exciting but daunting prospect for any newcomer, and potentially overwhelming for a young, single woman from the Maritimes who had grown up on a farm or in a small village. What may have made the transition easier was the sense of familiarity that many Maritimers felt towards the New England region and its major city. Since the eighteenth century, when first the Planters and then the Loyalists had migrated from New England to Nova Scotia and New Brunswick, the two regions had experienced close economic relations, cultural affinities, and frequent cross-border migrations. By the second half of the nineteenth century, many of the small Maritime towns had direct links with Boston through the coastal trade. Even after the end of Reciprocity, Maritimers continued to export their farm produce and fish to Boston and to import manufactured goods, often through small-scale transactions. According to Alan Brookes, "just about every [Maritime] community situated by water sent some kind of vessel to the Hub."[12] When ship's crews returned, they brought news of the city and of the thousands of Maritimers who lived there.[13]

The small vessels that plied the coastal waters between Maritime ports and Boston also occasionally carried passengers, and one such sailing craft brought Alice Peck to the city from Bear River, Nova Scotia. According to her son's recollections, in the summer of 1879 Alice went down to the wharf in Bear River, waited for a boat, and finally got passage on the two-masted schooner of Captain George Langley. He was on his way to Boston to sell farm goods and to purchase hay and flour for the lumber camps in the forests inland from Bear River.[14]

In addition, by the 1880s a railroad connected Boston to lines throughout the Maritimes, and commercial steamships plied the waters between the city and provincial ports, offering a less expensive alternative to the rails[15] (see figure 3). The 1878 *Boston City Directory* listed steamship departures to Saint John, Digby, Windsor, Halifax, and Charlottetown on Mondays, Wednesdays, and Fridays; to Yarmouth and Saint John on Tuesdays; and to Halifax, Port

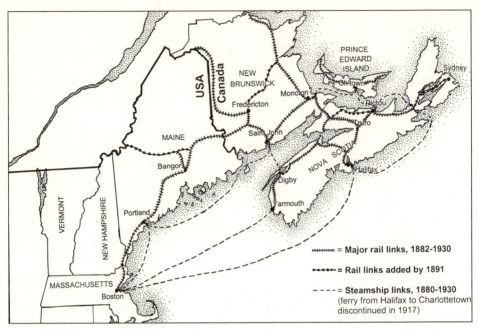

Figure 3
Commercial transportation links between the Maritime provinces and Boston, 1880–1930

Hawksbury, Pictou, and Charlottetown on Saturdays. The announcements also mentioned connecting service to inland communities like
Fredericton and "all stations on the Intercolonial."[16] With frequent
service to many Maritime locations the steamships became, in historian Arthur Johnson's words, "prime carriers" for many forms of
cargo, from perishable goods to immigrants.[17]

FINDING A JOB

However they travelled to Boston, upon arrival all but the few fortunate woman with positions waiting for them faced the immediate
necessity of finding housing and work. Both were crucial, but securing employment was paramount because the type of occupation one
found – the nature and location of the work and the wages it paid –
often determined the choice of lodging. Furthermore, a newcomer
might be able to afford a few nights in a hotel or might have friends
in the city who would house her for a short time, but most of the
young migrants had left households where cash was scarce and did
not have much money. It was critical that they find a job as quickly
as possible.

Knowing where to look for work was the first step in this process, and there were several ways that a Maritime migrant could obtain such information. Women who had contacts in Boston could ask fellow Maritimers if they either knew of available jobs or could offer advice from their own experiences. For other new arrivals, including Phebe Ann Sinclair of Flume Ridge, New Brunswick, the Young Women's Christian Association (YWCA) was the first institution they turned to for lodging and for guidance in finding employment.[18]

Founded in 1866, the Boston YWCA played a major role in both housing and job placement for single women who came to the city from rural North America and from Europe. According to its constitution, it was one of the association's duties to "seek out young women taking up their residences in Boston, endeavor to bring them under moral and religious influences, by aiding them in the selection of suitable boarding places and employment."[19] In keeping with this purpose, the YWCA over time built several boarding houses and established an employment bureau where Boston families seeking domestic servants of good character could find listings of acceptable applicants. In the 1880s the association created two more departments to serve the needs of both female immigrants and the city's employers: a Traveller's Aid program, consisting of YWCA workers who greeted young women arriving on boats and trains and provided information about the association's services, and a Business Register, which found employment for young women as seamstresses, sales clerkes, and service workes in hotels and public institutions.[20] As Fiona Bellerive has documented, for many single Maritime women arriving in Boston the YWCA was a welcoming place and a source of enormous help in getting safely established in the city.

But the association was not the answer to urban acclimation for all Maritime newcomers. For one thing, according to Bellerive, its Employment Bureau required three letters of reference before it would place a prospective domestic with a family.[21] As a result the bureau was more useful to women seeking to change positions than to new arrivals.[22] Another barrier that likely limited the numbers of Maritime women who used the YWCA as an employment agency or place to board was that the association was a Protestant institution with clearly stated evangelical goals. As its founders declared in their statement of purpose, an active member had to be a "Christian woman who is a member in regular standing of an Evangelical Church." Its calling was to "endeavor to bring" young women "under moral and religious influences."[23] Bellerive has pointed out that the association's Employment Bureau served Catholic as well as

Protestant women; in fact, until 1900 it did not make any note of the religious affiliations of its applicants in its records.[24] Nevertheless, the evangelical nature of the institution was well known, and more than a few Catholic and non-evangelical Protestant Maritimers likely found its proselytizing a source of alienation rather than support.

For them, and for others unaware of the usefulness of the YWCA, the process of finding work was a challenge. Migrants who had worked in Maritime cities before coming to Boston could apply what they had learned when looking for work in Halifax, Saint John, or Charlottetown to their search. Women with no other leads or affiliations in the city soon discovered that there were two principal places to find job openings: newspaper advertisements and commercial employment agencies.

Perusing want ads probably seemed the easiest and cheapest approach to job hunting. Newspapers like the Boston *Evening Transcript* were good sources for leads. But reading through the advertisements quickly revealed the drawbacks of finding employment through the newspaper. First of all, want ads were a more popular vehicle for those looking for work than for employers, so for every help-wanted listing there were two advertisements for women seeking positions. Those placing want ads were usually changing jobs; they could offer a potential employer both experience and references that the new arrival might not have. The following notice in the 15 July 1878 *Evening Transcript* was typical: "WANTED – By a competent seamstress a situation to do plain sewing or dressmaking; would go out by the day; No objections to the country; Address: Seamstress: 45 Lawrence Street."[25] This ad pointed out another problem with newspaper job searches for recent migrants: without a home-base they had no place to conduct an interview with a prospective employer who preferred to meet an applicant at her lodgings.[26] Finally there was the issue of religion. Although Irish women provided the largest single source of domestic servants in Boston, most who placed advertisements for servants in newspapers made it abundantly clear that they would consider only Protestant applicants.[27] The following item captures a common theme of help-wanted ads for domestics: "WANTED – A Protestant girl (none other) to do general housework. References required. Apply at No. 40 Woodbine Street, Boston Highlands, from 9 till 2."[28] Thus, many of the same Maritime newcomers who might have avoided the YWCA did not find newspaper want ads a useful means of finding work either.

The alternative for these women was to use the services of an employment agency, or what was sometimes referred to as the "intelligence office."[29] Historian David Katzman described these institutions as "the primary marketplace for urban domestic jobs," and if sheer numbers are indicative, they played a major role in job placement for Boston's working women.[30] The 1878 *Boston City Directory* listed twenty-three separate employment offices run by women and likely to have served the needs of female job applicants.[31] There were disadvantages to utilizing the services of the intelligence office, chief among them being the fee, which ranged from 10 to 25 per cent of the first week's wages, according to Katzman's figures.[32] Some mistresses, wanting to establish a personal, maternal relationship with their domestic servants, did not like the impersonal, market-oriented aspects of dealing with an intermediary.[33] And not all employment agencies were reliable, even reputable. They did not always give an honest account of working conditions in a prospective place of employment and sometimes demanded bribes. There were even reports in some cities that agencies acted as procurers for prostitution.[34] In spite of these objections, the intelligence office remained an important institution for matching female job-seekers with employers and, for newcomers to the city, a valuable way to enter the job market.

One way or another, the great majority of Boston's single, Maritime-born women found work. In the 1880 US census for the city, over 3,700 of them reported some type of paid employment, and among the 430 who did not were 42 in the hospital, who may have had jobs when healthy. Table B.1 in appendix B is a compilation of the occupations, combined into larger occupational groupings, of single Maritime women who were working in Boston in 1880. It is a long list of ninety-four separate jobs and eleven categories, but a glance at the figures in each category reveals that one type of employment was the preponderant choice of these women. Over two-thirds of the women were employed in just eight occupations that fall under one umbrella heading, domestic service (see table B.1). The only other occupational categories that attracted more than 10 per cent of the women were: institutional service, in which the large majority worked as domestics in boarding houses; and the sewing trades. Taken together, domestic and institutional service accounted for over three-quarters of all work pursued by single Maritime women in Boston. Most of these migrants, like their compatriots still living in the Maritimes, had learned household and sewing skills at home, and when they came to the city they looked for work that required these abilities.

Besides the training they brought to the job, Maritime women had other compelling reasons for entering domestic service. One was the relative ease of finding a position. In nineteenth-century America, domestic service was the largest single source of employment available to women.[35] According to one estimate, in 1870 fully half of all working women in the United States had been a household servant at one time in their lives.[36] And, in growing cities like Boston, an expanding middle class meant an ever increasing demand for domestics, leading to the perennial complaint among wealthier families that there were never enough good servants to go around.[37] In 1880, throughout the metropolitan centres of the United States, domestic service was a seller's market.

Another attractive aspect of household service for some single Maritime-born women was the quality of housing conditions. A servant often worked in surroundings far more elegant than those in which she had grown up. Coming from rural farmhouses or working-class homes in the Maritimes, many women found themselves living for the first time in houses with indoor plumbing, running water, gas lighting, and comfortably furnished surroundings. While individual conditions varied from household to household depending on both the wealth and the generosity of the family, most live-in servants could expect cleaner, safer, and more comfortable living quarters than the rooms they could afford to rent on a typical working woman's wages.[38] Besides, if one situation was unsatisfactory, a servant could simply leave and look for another job, a common practice for late-nineteenth-century American domestics in a labour market where demand always exceeded supply.[39]

Nevertheless, to some women, particularly native-born white women with other occupational options, the disadvantages of domestic service outweighed any advantages, and each year the proportion of working women entering service declined.[40] One serious drawback to domestic service was the live-in domestic's lack of free time. All servants shared the common experience of days that began before sunrise and ended well after the evening meal. Even during the few slack periods in a servant's day, she was "on call" and could not leave the house. In his book *Seven Days a Week: Women and Domestic Service in Industrializing America*, David Katzman also noted that while by the 1880s most urban and government employees worked five and a half days, with Saturday a "half-holiday," the time off allotted to the average live-in servant was only "part of Sunday and one other night a week."[41] Moreover, in the eyes of many wage-earning women, the worst aspect of domestic service was the social stigma attached to the job.[42] The attitude of one factory-worker-turned-domestic was typical: "Very slowly, I buttoned my apron, the badge of the servant. I knew Minnie and Sadie and all the other girls who worked in shops and factories would stop associating with me. I had dropped out of their class."[43]

Thus, single, Maritime-born women who came to Boston in the late nineteenth century willingly took the jobs that many American women scorned. Why? What can this choice reveal about the role that migration and employment played in their lives? Again the examples of Clara and Alice Peck are instructive. Both women left home in order to help support their father's farm in Bear River. The adventure of such a trip may have excited them – the chance to see a large city, meet new people, earn their own wages – but their primary motive for leaving home was filial responsibility, not personal desire, a motivation that likely was common to the majority of Maritime-born single women in Boston. And, for single women whose primary goal was to save money to send to their families back home, there was no more suitable work than some form of household service. For one reason, in return for long hours of labour a domestic made wages high enough to enable "the thrifty to save respectable sums of money."[44] For another, domestic service allowed workers to save the greatest share of their earnings not only because the job included room and board but because it left women so little time off to spend money.

The employment patterns of single women immigrants from other countries mirrored those of the Maritimers. Single women from throughout Europe entered household service for some of the same reasons that likely motivated Maritime women: availability of work, quality of living conditions, decent wages that included room and board.[45] At least for single Irish women in the United States, the ability to save money to send back to their families in Ireland was the single most important rationale for becoming a live-in servant.[46] Sending money home was the established behaviour of young, single women in nineteenth-century western Europe who left rural families to work in larger cities.[47] Redefining the structures of the traditional family economy to include urban wage work for daughters – most often as domestics – was a common strategy of households anywhere that industrial capitalism acted to transform both rural and urban economies.

Yet not every young woman from the Maritimes who worked in Boston in 1880 was a domestic servant. Some were saleswomen; others became nurses; a few found clerical positions; and over one in six ended up in one of the sewing trades. Were these women also able to save money to send back to families in New Brunswick, Nova Scotia, and Prince Edward Island? According to the calculations of Carroll Wright, statistician for the Massachusetts Bureau of Statistics of Labor in the 1880s, it would have been difficult for any working woman in Boston who had to pay for her room and board to accumulate any savings. In his study of working women in Boston in 1883, Wright sampled 1,032 women who laboured in the city. He averaged their annual income to $269.07 and, for the 959 who paid for their room and board, their annual living expenses to $261.30. The difference was "a margin for everything outside of the absolute necessaries of life of $7.77."[48] With such a narrow gap between wages and cost of living, it is not surprising that, of the 959 women paying their own room and board, only 120 had managed to save any money in the previous year and 30 had gone into debt.[49]

The so-called needle trades were notorious in American cities for paying "starvation wages" and offering unsafe working conditions.[50] Yet, there are several reasons why these conditions may have been somewhat less onerous for Maritime women in Boston, at least before 1890. First, although the specific occupational titles that women gave to census takers were not always consistent, there were differences among the various jobs that fell under the general category of "sewing trades." Thus, at least some of the women who claimed to be tailoresses and worked in a shop, or for a men's clothing establishment, may have commanded relatively higher wages, depending on their skills and experience, than sewing-machine operators who worked in factories for an average weekly wage of $6.62.[51] In addition, some women who listed their occupation as seamstress worked for a single family and lived with them as a servant, thus obviating the costs of room and board.

Second, research done by Carolyn McCreesh on American women garment workers reveals that Boston offered women in the sewing trades "somewhat better working conditions" than those available in the other leading industrial cities, New York, Philadelphia, Chicago, and Baltimore.[52] Before the 1890s, when home-based piece work was introduced, clothing production in the city took place in factories and paid an average wage of $6.00 per week. Specialized workers such as milliners and vest makers earned an average of $7.97 and $9.00 per week, respectively. These rates were not generous, but neither were they "starvation wages" and they far exceeded the $4.85 average weekly wages paid to female workers in the textile trades. Even the boot and shoe factories of Boston paid lower average weekly wages than the garment trades – $5.04. To earn more money for shoe work, one had to look for employment in Lynn.[53] Thus, it is possible that some of the 666 single Maritime-born women working the sewing trades in Boston could have afforded to send small sums of cash back home. And even those daughters who could afford to support only themselves may have helped their families just by being financially independent.

LIVING CONDITIONS

For those single Maritime women who worked in domestic or institutional service and had room and board provided, finding housing was not a concern. However, those woman who found jobs in the needle trades, or in factories, or as saleswomen, faced the additional problem of finding decent and affordable lodging. As with employment, one place to begin might have been the newspaper want ads, where, in the summer of 1878, new arrivals would have found listings such as, "113 Salem Street. To let, one large front room, nicely furnished; let cheap; the best locality at North End,"[54] or, "Board and Rooms – Two unfurnished rooms, up one flight, with board, at 45 Upton Street (first house from Tremont Street."[55] Listings such as these, usually for rooms in boarding or lodging houses in the North, West, and especially the South End of the city, attracted increasing numbers of single working men and women as the nineteenth century neared its end.[56] Offering varying levels of independence from parental-like controls (some requiring sit-down meals with other boarders and evening curfews, others no supervision at all), such living arrangements held out the opportunity for single youths to try out life either partially or totally on their own. According to Carroll Wright's research, some of the "working girls" of Boston did live in such housing in 1883, although only through "very close economy" of their earnings.[57]

However, a review of the choice of living arrangements of single female Maritimers in Boston reveals that, in 1880, most were not likely to be living in such unregulated situations. Instead, more than 400 of these women lived with some relative, and over 500 more boarded with a single family (see table 4). According to John Modell and Tamara Hareven, in their study of boarding and lodging in late-nineteenth-century Boston, boarding with another family was a common practice of mutual benefit to both boarder and host family. The household gained another source of income while the boarder, "usually young and with shallow resources," learned "the ways of the city" in a "quasi-familial setting."[58] By contrast, only 366 of these women lived in the more impersonal setting of a boarding house.

By far the most common housing arrangement for single Maritime-born women was as a servant in another household. That so many chose this most controlled of all living situations reinforces the idea that a majority of these women were not seeking an escape from

Table 4
Relationship to head of household of single Maritime women in Boston, 1880

Relationship to head of household	Number	% of total*
Head	126	3.0
Sister	187	4.5
Sister-in-law	123	3.0
Niece	85	2.0
Aunt, cousin, other relative	30	.7
Boarder, private home	543	13.1
Boarder, boarding house	366	8.9
Servant	2,697	64.9
Total	4,157*	100.1**

Source: US Census of Population, 1880, Schedule no. 1: Boston, Suffolk County, Massachusetts, in US National Archives and Records Service, *Tenth Census of the United States, 1880* (Washington: NARS, 1960), reels 552–62.

  * Total does not include 9 cases where information on relation to head of household was illegible or missing in the census.
** Does not add up to 100 percent because percentages are rounded off.

adult authority. Since they were the first generation of daughters from the region to leave home in significant numbers while still young and single, it is not surprising that they did not immediately embrace independent living (or perhaps that their parents discouraged such behaviour). In fact, the tendency to continue living as a subservient member of a household was common among the first generation of single women who went to work in nearby urban areas in nineteenth-century western Europe, according to Joan Scott and Louise Tilly, and is indicative of the preservation of traditional pre-industrial family relationships in an urban, industrialized setting.[59] Thus, domestic service appeared a doubly ideal job for the Maritime daughter in the city: it offered decent pay with few expenses, and it transplanted the young woman from one family setting to another.

There was an irony in this transplant. When a young woman left her Maritime family for another household, she traded the familiar for the unknown and, too often, social connections for isolation. Unlike migrants who came to Boston as families and settled together in certain districts, single Maritime women ended up scattered all across the city, usually living with strange families rather than with their cohort. Table 5 indicates the ward-by-ward distribution of single female Maritimers in Boston in 1880. These women lived in varying numbers in each of the city's twenty-five wards. The only ward in which more than 10 per cent were congregated was Ward 11, the area that included the wealthy Back Bay, where families often had more

Table 5
Distribution by ward of single Maritime women in Boston, 1880

Ward	Number	%
1	139	3.3
2	117	2.8
3	56	1.3
4	61	1.5
5	105	2.5
6	86	2.1
7	101	2.4
8	101	2.4
9	311	7.5
10	234	5.6
11	675	16.2
12	167	4.0
13	36	.9
14	130	3.1
15	74	1.8
16	187	4.5
17	286	6.9
18	332	8.0
19	82	2.0
20	121	2.9
21	288	6.9
22	65	1.6
23	134	3.2
24	244	5.9
25	34	.8
Total	4,166	100.1

Source: US Census of Population, 1900, Schedule no. 1: Boston, Suffolk County, Massachusetts, in US National Archives and Records Service, *Tenth Census of the United States, 1880* (Washington: NARS, 1978), reels 676–89.

than one servant, and sometimes as many as ten or eleven. In those families there was often more than one domestic worker from the Maritimes, sometimes – as with Clara and Alice Peck – more than one member of the same family. But these young women were not typical. Most domestics were the only servant in a family and faced the adjustment to a new family, a new city, and a new country alone.

Exacerbating the isolation of these migrants were the long hours that they worked. As a rule, domestics had only Thursday night and part of Sunday off, and if a mistress were planning to have company on Sunday, even the latter could be lost.[60] Women in the clothing trades usually had their evenings free but, in periods of high production, if they could not finish their allotted work during the working day, they were expected to finish it at home that night.[61] Long hours and, in the case of boarders, little extra money meant that these migrants had few opportunities to socialize with friends or meet young men.

Yet census data suggest that young Maritime women did manage to meet young men. In 1880 2,242 of the Maritime-born women living in Boston were married to men from outside the Maritime provinces; an additional 1,484 were married to Maritime-born men.[62] Some of the latter couples undoubtedly came to Boston after marriage, but others likely met and married while in the city.

One of the few times and places that young Maritimers, even servants, could meet was at church services. Alice Peck met her future husband, John Edgar McKay, at the adventist church in Roxbury. A ship's carpenter who worked in East Boston (Wards 1 and 2), John would have had no opportunity to encounter the Peck sisters had they not attended the same church and participated in activities there. Although solid evidence is sparse, it is probable that many other young Maritime women found not only social contacts but spiritual comfort at their local churches. One daughter reported that her mother, working as a cook in Boston in the 1890s, had attended "the big Churches" and had been "privileged to hear some of the great Evangelists of that day, Moody, Spurgeon, Talmadge and Gypsy Smith."[63] Many of the migrants from Cape Breton gathered at the United Presbyterian Church in the South End, which, in the last decade of the nineteenth century, featured pastors from Cape Breton and "fine Gaelic sermons preached in its frequent Gaelic services."[64] Attendance at church services and participation in church functions were the kinds of wholesome activities acceptable for a woman living in even the most controlling household, and they offered the young Maritimer a chance to get away from the demands and constant subservience that all woman's work – whether in a home, shop, or factory – demanded. Within the confines of religious teachings that reinforced the ideology of female subservience, church attendance provided these migrants the opportunity for a modicum of freedom and a chance to meet other youths, often other Maritimers.

The other important escape from the routine of work for these migrants was summer vacation. Vacations were not paid, nor were they always voluntary. Summer was the slack season for most manufacturing and sales work; according to Carroll Wright, work was so hard to find in the summer that some women left the city to find work as table girls in seaside and mountain resorts.[65] But another alternative for the Maritime daughter temporarily without work was to return home and help with family needs in return for room and board until work in Boston picked up in the fall. Less disruptive than seeking other employment and less expensive than surviving without an income, it was the most likely option for these women, providing their families were willing and able to support them.

Domestic service, by contrast, was year-round work. Still, it was apparently common practice for Maritime-born servants to return home for at least part of the summer to help their families, either with the blessing of their employers or with the intention of seeking another position in the fall. For example, Phebe Ann Sinclair, who worked as a cook in Boston in the 1890s, returned home to Flume Ridge, New Brunswick, for two months each summer to help her mother with household chores.[66] Although both Alice and Clara Peck lived and worked in Boston, neither was listed in the city's 1880 census, because it was taken in the summer, when the two were in Bear River helping their father on the farm.[67] As the example of the Peck sisters illustrates, the census undoubtedly underreported single Maritime-born women in the city because a number were visiting families in Canada when the census was taken.

Evidently employers got used to the idea of having their Maritime maids leave them to return home for the summer, as is evident in the letter one mistress wrote to her former servant, Lillian Wentzel, in the early fall of 1905. In the letter the employer, Mary A. Sheldon, asked whether Lillian would be coming back to her employ, and, in apparent response to Lillian's query, stated that both of Lillian's sisters would likely be able to find similar positions in the area. Mrs Sheldon wrote: "It is the time now, when people are coming to their homes from the country and the seashore and I do not believe it would be a difficult thing for either of your sisters to find places," implying that many families had not had their full complement of servants during the summer.[68]

Thus, for most single Maritime women, time outside work was limited and devoted primarily to church activities and vacations spent helping the family back home. Where, then, did the Maritime newspapers get the idea that single women who went to Boston were in great moral danger? Was there any truth to the cautionary tales of women who, unable to survive in the big city or tempted by its pleasures, ended up seduced and abandoned or "on the busy thoroughfares in the evening"?[69] Or were these reports merely hyperbole, attempts to scare the daughters of the Maritime provinces, and their parents, into reconsidering plans to migrate to Boston? The answer lies some place between the two extremes. In the context of the over 4,000 single Maritime-born women in the city, the number whom society would have branded "fallen" – who were openly sexually active, became prostitutes, or bore illegitimate children – was probably small. Even allowing for the secrecy surrounding such behaviour, there is little surviving documentation to suggest that Maritime women were disproportionately prone to violating societal norms of female sexual purity. But some did get caught violating these norms, and some among them may have been as much victims of sexual exploitation by family members, employers, or fellow employees as wilful deviants from contemporary moral standards.

One result of violating sexual standards was the birth of an "illegitimate" child. There is no way of knowing how many single Maritime women became pregnant while in Boston, but it did happen, as Annie M. Baker and Mary J. McLean could have testified. Both were patients in the New England Hospital for Women and Children at the time of the 1880 census, and each had given birth to a child known only as "baby Baker" and "baby McLean," respectively. Both listed their occupation as servant, suggesting the possibility that the father might have been a member or acquaintance of the families for whom the women worked, particularly since servants were so often isolated from their own peers. Whoever the father was, unless the result was marriage, a young single woman with a baby faced a very difficult future. Some families may have hired a mother as a servant, along with her child, but because the child was a distraction from a domestic's primary responsibility to the mistress and a visible sign of a servant's immorality, such hirings were undoubtedly rare. And it was virtually impossible to hold a job in a shop or factory six days a week with a baby at home, unless the mother had a friend or relative willing to care for the child during working hours.

The solution for the single mother was to bring the child back to the Maritimes and leave it with her family, or another family willing to care for it, while she continued working. One women from Cape Breton described her sister's plight. She had been working in Boston when she met and married a man who, unbeknownst to her, had another wife. When the sister became pregnant, the other wife reported the polygamous husband to the police, and the sister had to sign a paper annulling her marriage. Left with a child, she returned to Cape Breton, where her parents took care of the baby.[70] In another case, a man, who for personal reasons wished to remain anonymous, reported that in his community in New Brunswick a young single woman who had gone to work in Boston, gotten pregnant, and had a child, brought the baby home to her parents and then returned to the city. The parents raised the child as their own and eventually adopted it.[71] Thus, if a single mother was fortunate enough to have, or know, a family willing to take in her baby, she could continue to work and help support her child. But even these women faced the painful prospect of leaving their offspring in the hands of others in order to retain their employability and a degree of respectability.

On the other hand, some Maritime women, either by choice or in desperation, abandoned all pretence of social respectability and became prostitutes. As with illegitimacy, it is impossible to know how many Maritime-born women took up prostitution in the 1870s and 1880s. However, research by Barbara Meil Hobson on prostitution in nineteenth-century Boston included a ten-year analysis of 1,030 women arrested and incarcerated in the Boston House of Correction for soliciting sex. This study, which included place of birth of inmates, indicates that between 1856 and 1865, 100, or 9.8 per cent, of these women were born in Canada.[72] Given the proximity of the Maritime provinces to Boston, it is likely that many of these women were from that region, and, by extension, that an even larger number were in the trade during the 1870s and 1880s, when more single Maritime women were in the city.

Augmenting Hobson's research is the discussion of prostitution that Carroll Wright included in his study of working women in Boston in 1883. He interviewed 170 women prostitutes in "houses of ill-repute" known to the city police department, and although he did not ask their places of birth, he did obtain information about the work they had done before prostitution and their motives for taking up the trade. Of the 170, 60 had been servants either in homes or institutions, 32 came from textile factories, 5 from shoe factories, 19 from some type of sewing trade, 6 from sales situations, 18 from various occupations, and 30 had no previous employment.[73] The women gave various reasons for entering prostitution: 59 became prostitutes "by choice, most of them on account of love of easy life and love of dress," 46 entered "through seduction," 26 because of "poor pay and hard work," and 17 because of "ill treatment at home." Twenty-two women declined to give a reason.[74] These responses are revealing because, behind the moralistic tone of phrases like "the easy life" and "love of dress," is a picture of women tired of long hours of hard work, frustrated by low pay, and constantly faced with temptation or exploitation by men who may have wielded power over them (as is possible for the sixty who had previously been servants).

Whatever the reasons for entering prostitution, the decision put women at risk of more than just societal condemnation. Venereal disease was an ever present danger. In one study of prostitution in New York in the 1850s, William Sanger found that two-fifths of the women had contracted syphilis or gonorrhea at one time in their lives.[75] While rarely fatal, according to Hobson's research, venereal diseases were debilitating and could cause infertility.[76]

Fear of disease, of social ostracism, and of personal shame led some women to leave the profession. Others were taken out forcibly when they were arrested and confined to the Boston House of Correction. Still others were "rescued" by a moral reformer or released from prison and sent to an institution established to rehabilitate the "fallen woman." One such woman was Emily Murphy, a twenty-one-year-old from New Brunswick, who, at the time the 1880 census was taken, was incarcerated in the Penitent Female Refuge. Founded in 1821, the refuge was designed on the model of the antebellum asylum; it isolated its inmates from society to remove them from the temptations of the outside world and structured their lives around work and prayer.[77] More comfortable than the House of Correction, the refuge was still a form of imprisonment for the women behind its walls, an imprisonment even more desolate for a young immigrant far from home and treated like a pariah.

But women such as Emily Murphy and the other Maritime-born prostitutes in Boston were likely a small minority of the single female Maritimers living in the city in 1880. Coming to a large city for the first time, often alone, these women were ideal candidates for sexual exploitation, yet few succumbed. In fact, the composite picture of the single female Maritimer in Boston was quite the opposite – that of a gainfully employed young woman, usually as a domestic in the household of a middle- or upper-class family, carefully accumulating savings and, when possible, sending money home to help with family expenses. In most cases these daughters left home to find work out of necessity, to augment the family's funds when economic survival demanded increasing amounts of cash or to relieve a household of an extra mouth to feed at a time when a daughter's economic contribution at home was limited. Once in Boston, they lived simply, working most of their waking hours, and residing, in most cases, in the supervised setting of another family. What social life they had often centred on church attendance, and when they took time off it was to return home and help with family needs. Thus, this first generation of single female migrants, sent to the city as part of a family strategy of adjustment to changing economic conditions in the Maritimes, in most cases responded to parental demands with the behaviour of a dutiful daughter.

Some of these daughters, like Clara Peck, remained in Boston most or all of their lives. Some married and stayed in the city, as demonstrated by the 1880 census data on Maritime-born women married to non-Maritimers. Others returned home and lived the rest of their lives in the Maritimes. But all these women shared a common experience: they were part of a vanguard, the first group of single women to leave the Maritimes in large numbers and go to work in Boston, a cosmopolitan city of over 350,000 residents and a major industrial, commercial, and intellectual metropolis in North America. Although their individual lives were circumscribed by their living and working conditions, they all encountered an environment more sophisticated and cosmopolitan than any they had known before. Long after they had moved back to the Maritimes, or married, or moved to another place, they remembered their lives in Boston and relived them every time they recited anecdotes about those years to friends, relatives, and offspring. A new generation of Maritime daughters would grow up hearing these stories, and they would remember.

PART TWO
Eldorado

3 The Maritimes in the Early Twentieth Century

Jennie May Peck, the niece of Clara and Alice Peck, was born in Bear River, Nova Scotia, on 15 September 1905, one of ten children of Levi and Emma Peck. Like her two aunts, Jennie grew up on a farm, a mixed farm where her family raised "the usual vegetables," had fruit trees, and harvested the raspberries and blackberries that grew in the pasture. The farm produced food for the family as well as surpluses for the regional market, which probably included the larger port town of Digby. However, like his father before him, Levi could not support his family solely from the farm, and he augmented his income by working as the operator of Bear River's electrical power-house. Jennie's brothers and sisters worked as well: one brother went out West to help harvest crops on the large prairie farms; others cut wood in the nearby forests; and three siblings went to work in Boston, one brother as a taxi driver and two sisters as domestics. In October 1926 Jennie also left home and went to work as a domestic servant in Boston, sending money back to her family to help with expenses on the farm. Her contribution was significant. "We paid the mortgage off on the house," she revealed. "I think it was three hundred dollars. One sister and I."[1]

From the broad outlines of Jennie Peck's early life, it would appear that she followed the same path that her two aunts had blazed nearly fifty years earlier. A product of a farm family that required the wage contributions of all able-bodied members to support the family economy, Jennie dutifully left home, went to the closest major metropolis, and took a position that best enabled her to save money and contribute to the family coffers. Had nothing changed for the second generation of Maritime daughters who went to work in the Boston States in the first three decades of the twentieth century?

In fact, Jennie's life did parallel those of her aunts Alice and Clara in substantial ways, but a closer examination of Jennie's experiences reveals some important differences as well. First, Jennie was twenty-one when she left home, not sixteen as her Aunt Clara had been when she went to Boston. Before leaving and taking on responsibility for helping with family finances, Jennie had completed Grade 11 in school, or what was then the equivalent of a high school education. She also had held two jobs in the area, and neither had involved domestic work. After finishing school she worked at the Grand Central Hotel in Bear River for $3.00 a week and then served as a school teacher in the nearby Morganville elementary school for an annual wage of $385. When asked why she chose to leave these jobs to work in Boston, Jennie did not mention better job opportunities or the ability to earn more money for her family, although these may have been motives. Instead, she responded, "Well, my two sisters had already gone to Boston, so I wanted to go too." Individual desire as well as filial duty influenced her decision.

Once in the city Jennie became a maid in a private home, as her aunts had done earlier. However, she was apparently not satisfied with domestic service, whatever its advantages for saving money to send home; while working as a servant she also attended Burdett Business College. Her education reaped benefits when her employer, who was also an executive at a tool-making operation, "called up and wanted to know if I'd come in the office to work." Jennie went from domestic service to office employment, where she supervised the work of four other women, kept the payroll, counted industrial diamonds, and tested the hardness of metals that were sent to the office. She also moved from the home where she had been a servant and found a place to board nearby. In the latter years of her stay, she rented an apartment in Allston, a Boston suburb.

Like her aunts, Jennie Peck was a devout Adventist and attended the local Advent Christian Church on Warren Street in Roxbury. However, church activities did not take up all her free time, even in the years she was a domestic. Sunday afternoons were often spent with her sisters enjoying the floral displays at the Arnold Arboretum in West Roxbury or, in summer, on trips to Revere Beach or Nantasket Beach. All these places were easily accessible by Boston's public transportation system of street cars and subways. She also visited friends and relatives living in the city and mentioned "two or three boyfriends."

Table 6
Estimates of population change in the Maritime provinces and Canada, 1901–31
(in thousands)

Decade	Population and changes	Canada	New Brunswick	Nova Scotia	Prince Edward Island
1901	Population	4,101	251	354	79
1911	Population	5,528	265	378	74
1901–11	Natural increase	711	44	52	12
	Net migration	+715	−30	−28	−17
1921	Population	6,677	292	403	69
1911–21	Natural increase	1,036	52	62	9
	Net migration	+113	−25	−37	−14
1931	Population	8,169	310	402	69
1921–31	Natural increase	1,389	61	69	9
	Net migration	+103	−43	−70	−9

Source: M.D. Urquhart and K.A.H. Buckley, *Historical Statistics of Canada* (Toronto: Macmillan, 1965).

In spite of this busy social life, Jennie remained single for the thirteen years she worked in Boston – in her own words, "a fussy old maid ... looking for the perfect man." She also returned home each summer and eventually moved back permanently, reflecting in later years that "home was always Bear River." Three years after she returned, one of her sisters died, leaving a husband and four children. A short time thereafter, Jennie married her sister's widower, Wilbur O. Parker. In 1993 the two still lived on "Peck's Hill," land that had been owned by members of the Peck family for over a century.

ECONOMIC DECLINE AND CONTINUING OUT-MIGRATION

Four of the ten children of Levi and Emma Peck – three daughters and one son – travelled to Boston to find work in the early years of the twentieth century. According to migration figures for the Maritime provinces, these young people were just a tiny fragment of what had become a mass movement out of the region. Table 6, which compares estimated net migration statistics for each of the Maritime provinces with those for Canada in the first three decades of the twentieth century, reveals the divergent pattern of population movement for the region from the country as a whole. While Canada's population burgeoned from natural increase and from immigration,

Table 7
Maritime men and women in Boston, 1905 and 1915

	Men	Women	Sex ratio: males per 100 females
1905	12,232	17,601	69
1915	13,424	20,273	66

Source: Massachusetts, Bureau of Statistics of Labor, Census of the Commonwealth of Massachusetts, 1905 (Boston: Wright and Potter, 1908); Massachusetts, Bureau of Statistics of Labor, The Decennial Census, 1915 (Boston: Wright and Potter, 1918).

population in the Maritimes at best stagnated; in the case of Prince Edward Island between 1911 and 1921, the population actually declined. The chief factor determining the Maritimes' sluggish growth was out-migration.

Figures from the Massachusetts state censuses for 1905 and 1915 confirm that Boston remained a primary destination for these migrants (see table 7). They also reveal that Maritime-born women continued to outnumber their male counterparts in the city. The distribution of out-migrants in Levi Peck's family, with three of five daughters but only one of five sons going to Boston, was apparently as typical in the early 1900s as female-dominated rural-to-urban migration had been in the late 1800s.

Thus, the widespread out-migration of both men and women that began in the 1860s and 1870s continued unabated well into the twentieth century. This is not a surprising finding, because the conditions that had contributed to out-migration in the late nineteenth century – the policies and structural changes that undermined the region's mercantile economy, forced it into unequal economic competition with a wealthier, more industrialized central Canada, and eventually caused the decline of its indigenous industrial base – continued unabated into the twentieth century. More specifically, the forces of change set into motion in the late nineteenth century reached their full impact on the Maritime economy in the first decades of the twentieth century.

As noted earlier, one of the engines of this economic transformation was the National Policy, the system of protective tariffs and transportation policies created by the federal government to foster internal trade and a native industrial base. The construction of railroads connecting the Canadian provinces from coast to coast, combined with high tariff barriers to keep out foreign goods, realigned the patterns of economic activity in the Maritimes from international trade in traditional staples like timber and fish to industrial development. Throughout the 1880s local entrepreneurs built factories that manufactured an array of products including cotton cloth, woollen goods, rope, sugar, glass, paint and hardware, iron and steel.[2] By 1891, according to historian T.W. Acheson, "the industrial growth rate of Nova Scotia outstripped all other provinces in eastern Canada."[3]

By 1910 most of the industrial enterprises built by Maritimers under the protective umbrella of the National Policy were owned by corporations and investors outside the region.[4] Profits made in the Maritimes went to support industrial growth in central Canada, and corporate decisions were driven by what was good for the enterprise as a whole, not the local plant in Dartmouth, Sydney, or St Croix. Furthermore, central Canadian and international capitalists were not the only ones who preferred to invest their profits outside the region. Recent research on financial decisions made by the managers at the Bank of Nova Scotia have shown that, after a period of recession in the mid-1880s, these local financiers lost faith in local enterprises and increasingly invested the savings of Maritimers in central Canada.[5] The resulting outflow of capital exacerbated the imbalance between the capital-rich provinces of Quebec and Ontario and the capital-poor provinces of the Maritimes, leaving local industries less able to expand and even more vulnerable to outside takeover.

In retrospect, what happened to industrial development in the Maritimes after 1890 was not surprising. The tariffs that encouraged the creation of local industries in the region encouraged creation and expansion of industries in central Canada as well, and the east-west trade routes promoted by railway building and control of freight rates meant that central Canadian goods flowed easily into Maritime markets to compete with the region's manufactures. Many of the products made in Maritime factories were also made in central Canada, where larger establishments could manufacture more goods more cheaply. In the face of such competition, Maritime-owned enterprises were not likely to remain in local hands for long; either they would fail or be bought by central Canadian firms eager to remove competitors and take control of an industry. Moreover, by the early 1900s American and British financial interests also played a role in corporate takeovers of Maritime enterprises. In 1893 a group of businessmen from Boston, Montreal, and Nova Scotia leased most of Cape Breton's coal fields and formed the Dominion Coal Company. American interests took over another local company, Nova Scotia Steel and Coal, in 1917. Within three years, both companies has been purchased by a group of London capitalists and reformed into the British Empire Steel Corporation (Besco), thus placing the two largest mineral producers in the Maritime provinces under foreign control.[6]

In sum, by integrating the weaker Maritime economy to that of a stronger, more advanced industrial economy of central Canada, the National Policy contributed to the process of concentration of capital and control in the hands of corporate and financial elites in Quebec and Ontario. In time, the process took on an international cast as corporate interests in the United States and Great Britain invested in the region, making the most valuable industries vulnerable to outside takeover. Such predatory behaviour led the citizenry of the Maritime provinces to lose control over their own economic future.

This process was by no means uniform across the region, across the economic spectrum, or across time. Some industries flourished in one decade, only to decline in another; others continued to expand under outside ownership; still other sectors of the economy continued to be productive, but only in particular locations and under special circumstances. Still, for the region's workers the tenuous nature of Maritime enterprises undermined job security and made employment opportunities unpredictable. This insecurity alone was reason enough for many Maritimers to leave home.

OUT-MIGRATION AND WOMEN'S EMPLOYMENT OPPORTUNITIES IN THE MARITIMES, 1900–1930

The introduction of gender into an analysis of out-migration in the early 1900s weakens the direct link between decline of the region's indigenous industries and the departure of its youth. Job loss alone cannot account for the emigration of Maritime-born women who, if Boston's population statistics are indicative, continued to make up a large segment of the migrant stream in the early twentieth century. In fact, despite the region's severe economic problems, in several ways capitalist development in the Maritimes brought about an increase rather than a decrease in employment opportunities for young women.

First, some of the industrial enterprises that survived into the twentieth century, whether under local or central Canadian ownership, had a predominantly female workforce. For example, cotton mills and shoe factories in Yarmouth and Amherst, Nova Scotia, employed over a hundred women in each community in 1921.[7] Montreal interests assumed control of textile mills in the New Brunswick communities of Moncton, Marysville, and Milltown, near St Stephen,

Table 8
Men and women in the Maritime provinces living in rural and urban areas,* 1921

	Men	Women	Sex ratio: males per 100 females
Rural areas	327,729	302,034	108
Urban areas	180,991	189,991	95

Source: Sixth Census of Canada, 1921 (Ottawa: F.A. Acland, 1924–25).

* Urban areas are defined in the 1921 Canadian census as all cities, towns, and incorporated
  villages, regardless of size. Rural areas are those outside these locations.

but they remained in operation into the twentieth century and continued to hire female operatives.[8] Even in some of the small coastal communities, new employment opportunities for women became available when lobster- and fish-processing plants were built to accommodate a growing export market for seafood products.[9] However, factories usually drew their workforce from the local community and surrounding countryside, and there were many parts of the Maritimes that had neither a textile mill nor a lobster cannery, nor any other industry that employed women.[10] Thus, industrial labour was an important source of female employment, but only in specific parts of the region.

A more general impact of industrialization on job opportunities for female Maritimers was the urban growth that it generated. In the late nineteenth and early twentieth centuries the urban population in the Maritimes doubled while the rural population declined by 25 per cent.[11] In Nova Scotia alone, the proportion of the population that lived in urban settings – defined as all incorporated cities, towns, and villages – increased from 17.1 per cent in 1891 to over 35 per cent in 1911 and 45 per cent in 1931.[12] And, in 1921 as in 1871, females outnumbered males in the urban areas of the three Maritime provinces (see table 8). It is apparent from these figures that women from rural a reas continued to move into the cities and towns, presumably to find work.

While the pattern of female rural-to-urban migration persisted from the late nineteenth to the early twentieth century, employment options for women in urban settings changed significantly across this period. In 1871, fully 90 per cent of the female workforce were engaged in domestic service; in 1881, 1,752 women worked as servants in Halifax, a city of 36,100.[13] By 1931 domestic service still accounted for the largest number of female workers in the city, but while the population of Halifax had grown to 59,275, the number of female domestics totalled 1,274 – nearly 500 fewer than in 1881 – and represented just over one-fifth of the 6,188 female workers in the city. Saint John experienced a similar process of decline in numbers of female servants, from 1,057 in 1881 to 902 in 1931.[14]

Competing with domestic service for women workers by the early twentieth century was an array of new occupations generated by urban growth, technological advances, and the increasing scale and complexity of business enterprises. Boarding houses, lodging houses, hotels, and restaurants, built to house and feed migrants to the cities and towns of the region, sought housekeepers, cooks, maids, waitresses, and kitchen help.[15] An advertisement in the Amherst *Daily News* in June 1907 spread the word of such job openings: "GIRLS WANTED: One dining room girl, one chambermaid, and one that knows something about cooking; also one for kitchen. Wages from $9 to $15 per month for experienced help. Apply to Mrs. G.W. Benner, Cumberland House."[16] Even a community as small as Bear River had a hotel – it was here that Jennie Peck worked in the years before she went to Boston.

The declining rural population and growing towns and cities also altered the nature of teaching, long a female-dominated profession.[17] By the early twentieth century many rural schools had closed, and their districts were consolidated, transferring demand for teachers from the one-room country school to larger primary and secondary schools in urban areas.[18] Other social institutions such as hospitals, orphanages, asylums, and reform schools were established or expanded in this period, often in response to the poverty, overcrowding, and squalor of urban working-class districts.[19] These institutions provided work for many women, as matrons, maids, cooks, trained and untrained nurses, and other service personnel.

Many of these jobs – teaching, nursing, and domestic and institutional service, for example – were not new, but had become more plentiful with the growth of cities and towns. The most dramatic changes in employment options for women in this period, however, were the occupations that came into existence directly as a result of industrial capitalist development. Business consolidation, increased specialization in production, economies of ever greater scale, national and international markets, and technological advances all generated whole new categories of work.

One such category was office work. Once an entry-level job for young men seeking to learn a business, the position of office clerk was replaced in larger enterprises by a series of different jobs – secretary, bookkeeper, stenographer – that were all "dead-end," that is, unconnected to any track up the corporate ladder.[20] The middle-class young men who once had filled clerk positions quickly abandoned the field, leaving office employment to women at a time when it was expanding at an enormous rate. For women, virtually all of whom were denied career advancement because of their gender, office work meant higher wages and a more pleasant work environment than factory jobs, more independence than domestic or institutional service, and a degree of respectability usually reserved for professions like trained nursing. By the early twentieth century, women were rapidly filling available clerical positions in the offices of Maritime businesses.[21]

Another category of female employment to emerge from advanced industrial capitalism was sales. As more industries produced more consumer goods, the simple forces of supply and demand no longer guaranteed that a business would sell its products, so the latter years of the nineteenth century witnessed the birth of marketing techniques meant to convince consumers to buy new products regardless of need. Chief among these techniques were expanded and more sophisticated advertising, the development of brand loyalty, and above all, larger and fancier sales emporia.[22] Small drygoods stores were replaced by larger clothing establishments selling ready-made apparel. Variety stores that sold many products under one roof attracted shoppers who, looking for one item, might be tempted to purchase something else from another part of the store. Even the general store in the smallest hamlet often caught marketing fever and replaced small windows with floor-to-ceiling glass through which to display its wares. The polite, neatly dressed young ladies who stood behind counters and cash registers greeting customers and handling sales – and who worked for lower wages than men – were a key ingredient in the new sales strategy.[23] All across the Maritime provinces, young women found employment as sales clerks, and with the influx of national and international chain stores, these jobs multiplied.[24] According to L.D. McCann in his study of branch businesses in the region, by the 1920s, "the residents of Halifax, Truro, Sydney, New Glasgow, Moncton, or Saint John could, if they so chose, buy groceries at Dominion, shop for novelty items at a Steadman's or Metropolitan store, look for clothes at Tip Top Tailors, try on shoes at Agnew Surpass, or order all of these items from an outlet of T. Eaton and Company."[25]

Of all the employment opportunities for women to come out of industrial development and urbanization, none was more clearly the product of technological advances than the job of telephone operator. Telephone service in Canada was first established in the 1870s, and by the 1880s there were independent telephone companies in each of

Female telephone operators, New Glasgow, Nova Scotia, 1918 (From the MT&T Photograph Collection, Dalhousie University Archives. Photo courtesy of MT&T, Halifax)

the three Maritime provinces. From its inception, telephone transmission required intermediaries to handle connections between communicators, positions originally filled by young men, some no more than sixteen years old. Teenage boys soon proved unsatisfactory to company management – too "wild" and "undisciplined" – and within a decade most had been replaced by women, who, managers believed, would be more courteous to customers and more submissive to company rules.[26] By the early twentieth century, telephone service in the Maritimes had spread from the cities to smaller towns across the region, and a growing number of better-educated young women took positions at telephone switchboards, no doubt attracted by the image of telephone operators as the "elite of female clerical workers."[27] Wages for operators were somewhat less "elite," however; they were comparable to, and sometimes less than, what stenographers and other clerks received.[28]

Two apparent paradoxes emerge from this review of new employment opportunities for Maritime women in the early twentieth century. First, while the region was in the process of losing control over its economic development, jobs for women were increasing in both type and number. Second, despite unprecedented employment options in the region, women continued to emigrate. The first paradox is, perhaps, less contradictory than it appears. Women had always worked for lower wages than men, had rarely been allowed career expectations, and seldom had paid craft or work experience rendered obsolete by mechanization. Thus, some of the destructive forces of industrial capitalist development – deskilling of work, loss of workplace control, and restricted opportunity for advancement – did not affect them in the same way they affected men. Instead, the establishment of corporate monoliths, no matter who controlled them, meant a larger clerical staff, a bigger sales force, and more women handling telephone connections.

The more puzzling contradiction, and the one most germane to the study of female out-migration, concerns why, in the midst of an increase in work choices at home, so many women left the region. One partial explanation may be that the population of working-age women expanded at a faster rate than did the number of jobs. However, by the 1920s – when clerical and sales positions were most fully feminized – emigration (or negative net migration) actually exceeded the rate of natural increase in Nova Scotia, the most populous of the Maritime provinces (see table 6). It is likely that a female labour surplus, if it did exist, was not the only motive for emigration.

CONDITIONS IN THE RURAL MARITIMES AND FEMALE OUT-MIGRATION, 1891–1931

In the 1870s, at the beginning of the upsurge of out-migration from the Maritime provinces, the majority of Maritimers lived in rural communities and farmed, fished, cut wood, or combined two or three of these activities in order to make ends meet.[29] Competition for markets from larger farms farther west and increasing dependence on manufactured goods from central Canada necessitated an expansion of production and an increase in cash intake. Rural families' need for cash became a major reason for daughters to work for wages off the farm and go to the Boston States to find better-paying jobs that enabled them to send money back home. In the 1920s Jennie Peck migrated to Boston for precisely the same reason. Was she merely the last in a line of obedient-daughter migrants, or did young, single women from the rural Maritimes still flock to jobs in New England as a way to contribute to the family income? If so, were their sheer numbers enough to guarantee a constant stream out of the region, even as job opportunities for women proliferated in the Maritimes?

The idea that twentieth-century daughters emigrated as part of the extended family economy is predicated on several assumptions: that agriculture remained a major activity in the region, that rural families continued to depend on the contributions of most or all able-bodied members to prosper, and that most of the young, single women who left the region came from farms. Findings from literature on agriculture in the Maritimes after 1891 and from census data only partially support these assumptions.

In certain ways agriculture did remain a significant component of the Maritime economy. On Prince Edward Island it continued to be the cornerstone of the provincial economy.[30] In Nova Scotia the percentage of the export market held by agricultural products remained steady for the first three decades of the twentieth century in spite of increases in other materials such as coal.[31] And, from the 1890s to the 1930s – decades of significant urban growth – a large majority of the region's population still lived in rural areas.[32]

Nonetheless, in those same years the size of the rural majority steadily declined, from 84.1 per cent of the total population in 1891 to 62.2 per cent in 1931. Some of that decrease represented the migration of sons and daughters from farm families to cities and towns looking for wage work. In the 1890s, however, another component began to account for rural depopulation in the region as well: the wholesale abandonment of farms. Between 1901 and 1931 the number of farms in the three provinces declined from 105,232 to 86,334, a loss of 18,898.[33] The same forces that in the 1870s and 1880s had increased farmers' need for cash – competition for markets from larger farm operations in central and western Canada and increased dependency on manufactured farm implements, fertilizer, seed, and other products – intensified with technological advancements such as refrigerated transportation and the mechanization of agriculture. Refrigeration meant that perishable farm produce could travel farther, introducing more national and international competition.[34] At the same time, the introduction of ever more efficient – and expensive – farm equipment meant that the larger, more heavily capitalized farms of the North American Midwest, which had more modern machinery as well as more fertile soil, gained an even greater advantage over the smaller operations in the Maritimes.[35]

In the face of increased competition and the multiplication of farm costs, the Maritime farmers best able to survive were those who could produce for either a steady local market or a specialized international one. The result was an expansion of farm holdings in certain regions and the gradual abandonment of farms in others. Farms most likely to flourish were located in two distinct areas: those near urbanized areas and those with soils and climates suitable for production of one or two crops for which there was a particular demand. Farms most likely to fail were in areas best described as marginal, either because they were remote from population centres or because their geographic conditions limited the type and quantity of crops that could be cultivated.[36] Farming, once scattered throughout the provinces, increasingly clustered in certain regions, such as the Annapolis Valley and the Northumberland shore of Nova Scotia and the area around Sussex, New Brunswick. (Prince Edward Island remained predominantly agricultural across the province, but certain sections of Queens and Prince Counties did experience a greater expansion of improved land than other parts of the province.)[37]

But the right location was not the only requirement for a farm to prosper; it also had to produce marketable crops. A hallmark of successful agriculture in the early twentieth century was specialization, farms devoted to the cultivation of one or several commercially viable products. A review of agricultural census data for the first three decades of the twentieth century reveals that farmers responded to the challenge of competition by steadily reducing the production of certain crops – especially wheat, which could be grown more cheaply on the prairies – and increasing production of crops that were in demand and were better suited to one of the region's farming zones. Thus, by 1931, production of potatoes had risen dramatically, particularly in Prince Edward Island, where it became the most valuable cash crop of the province.[38] The production of dairy products also increased in the early years of the twentieth century, especially in regions like Kings County, New Brunswick, and Hants, Pictou, Cumberland, and Colchester Counties, Nova Scotia, all of which were close to growing cities and towns.[39] Perhaps the most famous example of specialized farming took place in the Annapolis Valley, where the gentle climate and fertile soils were ideal for the cultivation of apples. Orchards multiplied as farmers raised varieties of cooking apples that could withstand long-distance transport to the British market. At the peak, in the 1930s, Nova Scotia produced over 6,500,000 bushels of apples, virtually all of which were sent to the United Kingdom. The trade was so successful that its profits helped cushion the impact of the Depression across the Annapolis Valley.[40]

These, then, were the farms that prospered in the context of the capitalist transformation of agriculture: the ones that were fortunate enough to be situated on good soil or near urban markets; the ones large enough to produce profitable yields; the ones wealthy enough to have the mechanized equipment that ensured the most efficient

cultivation and harvesting. Nearly 19,000 farms did not fit these categories, and by 1931 they had been abandoned, their lands reverting
to forest, their inhabitants moved away. Among these inhabitants
were young women who likely needed work, and some of them may
have looked for jobs in urban centres, including Boston.

But the process of commercialization and specialization of agriculture was neither immediate nor absolute. Between the owners of
large, profitable enterprises on the one hand and the disinherited
farm families on the other were many who struggled along, trying
to hold on to their farms by whatever means possible. The Pecks
were one such farm family. According to Jennie, the family raised
crops such as vegetables and fruit both to eat and to sell; thus, theirs
was a mixed farm rather than a single-crop commercial venture.
Because the farm alone did not support the family of ten children,
Jennie's father, Levi, took outside work, following the region's long-
established practice of "occupational plurality."[41] In keeping with
another traditional rural pattern, all sons and daughters old enough
to find work earned wages – whether locally, out west, or in Boston
– to contribute to the family economy. In many ways, the means of
survival on the Peck farm were the same means used by farm families fifty years before, when daughters first began leaving home to
find wage work to help support the parental family.

But farm survival was increasingly difficult, as the over 18,000
farm failures between 1901 and 1931 reveal. In the case of the Peck
family, savings that Jennie and her sisters sent home were not spent
on farm implements but on mortgage payments on the farmhouse,
which had been used as collateral to borrow money to purchase
more land. In the face of competition from larger farms that produced crops strictly for commercial purposes, it became even more
difficult for small, mixed farms to continue. Many farmers, like Levi
Peck, responded by going into debt to buy land and expand their
operations. By 1931 over 14,000 farms in the Maritimes carried some
mortgage indebtedness.[42]

Adding mortgage payments to the increasing number of other
farm expenses – farm machinery and electricity, for example – meant
an even greater need for cash. In the case of the Pecks, all family
members old enough to find employment (except Jennie's mother)
worked for wages off the farm. The scattered evidence on rural families in the early-twentieth-century Maritimes suggests that the
Pecks' behaviour was common among rural families trying to hold
on to marginal farms. In Inverness County, Nova Scotia, for example,
the labour force in coal mines was only partly made up of permanent
workers; the rest were seasonal workers from nearby farms, "some

still with access to land and some means of subsistence," who worked in the mines in the hope of preserving their slim hold on independence.[43] At the same time, most of the young women who found work in the cities and towns of the region came from nearby rural areas.[44]

Apparently, in order to preserve their rural way of life, many farm families in the 1910s and 1920s still employed the nineteenth-century strategy of the family wage economy.[45] And, because daughters figured prominently in this strategy, it is possible that the majority of women who migrated to Boston in the early twentieth century – like Jennie Peck – were simply daughters following the examples of their mothers or aunts who went to the New England city to earn money for the family back home. Some of these daughters, like Jennie, may have worked in one of the Maritimes' newly created jobs for women before going to Boston, but they eventually left to seek better wages or steadier work.

Unfortunately, there is little more than sketchy information on the family backgrounds of Maritime women in Boston in the early twentieth century. From the over 14,000 women listed in the combined 1900 and 1910 censuses, it was possible to trace only 292 back to their parental families, and this small number included no New Brunswickers or women with especially common names.[46] Despite such limitations, information about these families is suggestive: 148, or 50.1 per cent, of the fathers were farmers; the next most common occupation was fisherman, the primary work of 26 fathers, or 9 per cent of the group. If these families are at all representative, then a significant percentage of the single, Maritime-born women in Boston in the early twentieth century had been raised on farms.

But what kind of farms were they? And were they all so marginal that their survival required the wages of daughters? It is virtually impossible to determine what was grown on each of the 148 farms or to assess their respective profitability. It is not even safe to assume that fathers who were farmers at the time of a daughter's birth or baptism still had their farms when that daughter was a young woman working in Boston. The only information that might even hint at the status of these farms is where they were situated. If they were located in regions with poorer soils or far from urbanizing areas, they would have been less likely to have prospered than those in zones more conducive to commercial agriculture. If this were the case, they would more likely have required off-farm income.

Table 9 groups by province and county the farms of Maritime-born women in Boston for whom fathers' occupations and places of birth could be ascertained. Two somewhat contradictory patterns emerge

Table 9
Location of farms of families of single Maritime women in Boston, 1901

Province and county	Number of farms
NOVA SCOTIA	128
Annapolis	6
Antigonish	10
Cape Breton	7
Colchester	12
Cumberland	8
Digby	2
Guysborough	2
Halifax	6
Hants	12
Inverness	11
Kings	15
Lunenburg	5
Pictou	18
Queens	4
Richmond	3
Shelburne	1
Victoria	3
Yarmouth	3
PRINCE EDWARD ISLAND	20
Kings	9
Prince	5
Queens	6
TOTAL	148

Sources: Nova Scotia Census, 1901, in National Archives of Canada, *Fourth Census of Canada*, 1901 (Ottawa: NAC, 1993), reels T-6446–T-6457; Prince Edward Island Census, 1901, in ibid., reels T-6509–6511.

from this limited body of information: that these women came from farms located in every county in Nova Scotia and Prince Edward Island, from the most fertile to the least hospitable for agriculture; and that the counties with the most farms were in regions where commercial agriculture was most likely to succeed. Hants, Kings, and Annapolis Counties, with a combined total of thirty-three farms, constitute the Annapolis Valley, home to Nova Scotia's largest and most productive apple orchards. Another large number of farms were clustered in the northern Nova Scotia counties near the Northumberland shore: Cumberland, Colchester, Pictou, Antigonish, and Inverness. This was an area of rich soils that supported several field crops like oats and barley as well as dairy farming.[47] It also included several growing towns – Amherst, New Glasgow, and Truro – as well as the steel-producing district around Stellarton and the coal-mining towns of Springhill and Inverness, all of which provided nearby markets for agricultural products. By contrast, there were only seventeen farms in the counties of Digby, Yarmouth, Shelburne, Queens, Lunenburg, and Guysborough, regions of heavily wooded uplands and rocky coasts, where the soils were thin and good arable land was scarce. Even Halifax County had only six farms, despite the presence of the large urban market of the cities of Halifax and Dartmouth. (The relatively even distribution of farms in Prince Edward Island fits the profile of a province with over 85 per cent of its land occupied as farms.)[48]

The Peck farm was one of only two in Digby County, a region of less than ideal conditions for agriculture. Not far from the community of Bear River the narrow band of good farm land receded into dense woods. But if the pattern of farm distribution described above is at all representative, then the Peck farm was not typical of those that other single Maritime women left when they went to Boston, and the reason Jennie Peck went to the city – to earn money for her family's farm expenses – was not necessarily what persuaded other female migrants to leave. For example, Katherine Inglis, a young woman who went to New England in the 1920s to train for nursing, was raised on a prosperous dairy farm in the Antigonish community of Lochabar. Without the burden of having to help defray farm expenses, she could afford to put pursuit of her own career ahead of family economic needs.[49] Thus, it appears that by the early twentieth century, motives for female out-migration were less frequently connected to a daughter's role in the family wage economy, though such traditional behaviour persisted in some families like the Pecks.

This exploration of the relationship between economic changes in the early-twentieth-century Maritimes and the continued emigration of single women has generated more questions than explanations. The connection, if it exists at all, seems filled with contradictions. In the midst of the region's economic decline and loss of control over its industrial development, employment options for women actually increased, so lack of job opportunities was less likely a motive for leaving than it had been in earlier years. On the other hand, rural depopulation meant surplus female workers entering urban labour markets and growing competition for these jobs; some of that surplus may have moved beyond Maritime cities to find work in the closest, most accessible metropolis, Boston. To bolster the relationship of rural depopulation to out-migration, there is some evidence to suggest that the majority of single Maritime-born women in Boston had been raised on farms. However, most of those farms were located in the very parts of the Maritimes most likely to have sustained farming in a time of transition from mixed production to monoculture and purely commercial agriculture. Farms in these regions were the least likely to have failed or require off-farm income to survive.

What begins to emerge from this conflicting information is a multi-faceted picture of female emigration – the possibility that in the twentieth century single women left the region for several reasons. This possibility, in turn, throws open a new set of questions about the nature of out-migration. Among second-generation migrants, was there no longer a correlation between family economic status and reasons for leaving home? If this were the case, was there no longer any similarity at all in the experiences and motives of those who emigrated? Or, did these women share common goals that do not surface when examining their behaviour only in terms of their relationship to their family's financial situation? Examining the economic changes in the Maritimes and their impact on single women in the early twentieth century has shed little light on these issues. To understand why so many of them left home it is necessary to follow them to Boston, to explore the work they did and the lives they led in a city much changed from the one their mothers' generation had known.

4 Working in Boston in the Early Twentieth Century

In October 1926 Jennie Peck left the family farm in Bear River, Nova Scotia, and came to Boston to enter domestic service in the Huston household. A decade earlier, Lulu Pearl Dempsey, from Stonehaven, New Brunswick, also travelled to the city to look for work, and found employment in a chocolate factory.[1] Two years after Jennie Peck arrived, Anita Saunders of Middleton, Nova Scotia, came to the city to begin training for a nursing career at McLean's Psychiatric Hospital.[2] During the same period Rhoda Hyson, of Oakland, Nova Scotia, took a job in a Boston book bindery; Louise Elizabeth Spidell, of Parkdale, Nova Scotia, sewed shirtwaists in factory; and Esther Campbell, of Milton Cross, Prince Edward Island, worked as a nanny for several families.[3] These women had much in common: their origins as Maritimers, their status as single women, and their intentions of finding work in the city. However, there is no evidence that any of these women ever met each other or were even aware of the others' existence. Where and how they lived in Boston were in large part defined by their occupation, and by the 1910s and 1920s work experiences were increasingly differentiated and isolated.

BOSTON'S ECONOMY AND JOB OPPORTUNITIES FOR WOMEN

Between 1900 and 1920 the city of Boston grew significantly in both size and number of residents. In 1916 the city annexed the town of Hyde Park and redrew its city limits and ward boundaries (see figures 4 and 5). As a result of this annexation and of continued in-migration from Europe and rural North America, its population grew from 560,892 to 748,060, a figure that did not include residents of surrounding communities such as Newton, Cambridge, Somer-ville, and Quincy.

Long a centre for mercantile activity – the hub city for New England's commerce – by the early twentieth century Boston had developed a more fully diversified economy that included light man-ufacturing of products from clothing to razors, a publishing industry, and a thriving service sector with particular strengths in the educa-tional, financial, and medical fields. The city's banks ranked fourth in the nation in the revenue they handled, behind only New York, Philadelphia, and Chicago.[4] Its institutions of higher education, from venerable Harvard University to the newer Massachusetts Institute of Technology, Boston University, and Boston College, attracted stu-dents and faculty from across the nation and beyond. Massachusetts General Hospital, Boston City Hospital, and Boston Lying-In Hospi-tal had long been considered among the finest such facilities in the country and had helped establish Boston's reputation as a centre for medical treatment and research. By the early twentieth century that reputation was reconfirmed with the construction of Peter Bent Brigham Hospital, Children's Hospital, the Collis P. Huntington Memorial Hospital, and the Beth Israel Hospital.[5] All these diverse economic activities generated city growth, evident in the expansion of downtown businesses, and spurred continued immigration of young men and women seeking employment.

Both the industrial and the service sectors of Boston's economy offered an especially large number of jobs for women, who outnum-bered men in the migrant stream of foreigners to the city.[6] Light manufacturing, particularly of clothing and shoes, employed many women, as did parts of the publishing industry such as printing and book binding. But, in close approximation to employment patterns for women in the Maritimes, it was in the growing professional, clerical, and mercantile fields that women's occupational opportuni-ties expanded most rapidly. In Boston, as elsewhere, women replaced men in low-level secretarial and sales work. The growth of the city and the influx of non-English-speaking immigrants from southern and eastern European meant increasing demands on the city's schools and social service agencies and employment for female teachers and social workers. The proliferation of hospitals and other medical services generated an unprecedented demand for nurses. And, though overshadowed by the growth of newer and more pres-tigious occupations for women, the demand for female household and institutional servants continued as well.

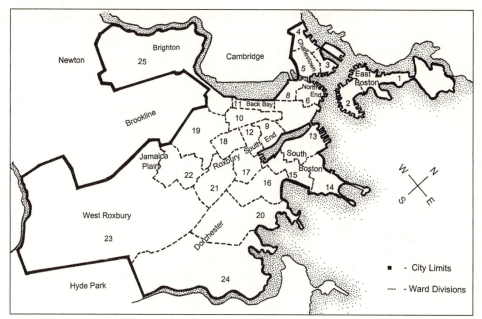

Figure 4
Boston, 1910, showing ward divisions

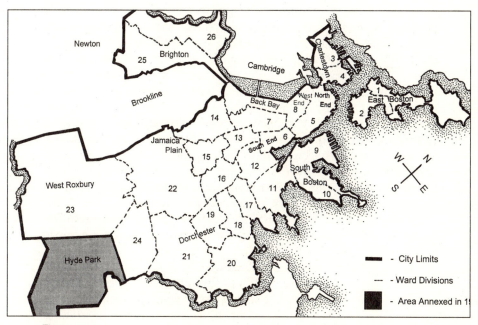

Figure 5
Boston, 1920, showing new ward divisions and areas annexed in 1916

Jennie Peck, Anita Saunders, Lulu Pearl Dempsey, and their cohorts joined thousands of single Maritime-born women who came to work in Boston in the first three decades of the twentieth century. It is impossible to state precisely how many of these women were living in the city in these years because none of the United States censuses after 1890 indicated a Canadian migrant's home province. However, figures from the Massachusetts state census for 1915 do separate those born in the Maritime provinces from other Canadian-born residents. Although no records exist just for single women, the ratio of all Maritime-born women to all other Canadian women in Boston was 20,273 to 25,732, or nearly 80 per cent of the total.[7] In light of these figures, it seems likely that a large majority of the single, English-Canadian women living in the city five years earlier were from the Maritime provinces, and that the behaviour of these women, as reconstructed from United States manuscript census data, can be construed to reflect the behaviour of women from the Maritimes. Comments by contemporary observers in Boston add anecdotal support to this assumption; the economist Frederick A. Bushee, for example, noted: "Looking first at British America, we find that the greater part of their emigration is from Nova Scotia alone."[8]

There were 7,325 single English-Canadian women living in Boston in 1910 and 5,258 in 1920.[9] The reason for the sharp decline in the number of these women in 1920 is not clear, but one factor may have been the economic conditions across North America and especially in the Maritimes. The end of the First World War in 1918 brought a simultaneous decline in employment and a rapid growth in numbers of job seekers as war production ceased and veterans returned home from Europe. The result was a deep depression, high unemployment, and serious labour unrest throughout the Maritimes. Wages were cut, workers were laid off, and strikes proliferated. According to historian Ian McKay, the Maritime provinces experienced at least ninety-three strikes in 1919 and 1920.[10] In these straitened times it is quite likely that emigration would dwindle, at least for a short while, until families could accumulate enough money for transportation. However, the decline was evidently short-lived: the 1920s proved to be the decade of greatest out-migration from the region, and throughout the period women headed to urban areas to find work.[11]

One aspect of life that did not change across the second decade of the twentieth century for single English-Canadian women in Boston was the expansion of employment options open to them. Tables B.2 and B.3 in appendix B list the occupations these women reported in the 1910 and 1920 United States manuscript censuses for Boston. In

Table 10
Types of occupations of single Maritime women, 1880, and single English-Canadian women, 1910 and 1920, Boston

Occupation group	1880		1910		1920	
	No.	(%)	No.	(%)	No.	(%)
Religious work	0	(.0)	82	(1.3)	112	(2.4)
Professional	83	(2.2)	855	(13.1)	862	(18.7)
Clerical	20	(.5)	522	(8.0)	506	(11.0)
Owner/manager – business	0	(.0)	206	(3.2)	153	(3.3)
Sales	56	(1.5)	273	(4.2)	230	(5.0)
Domestic service	2,428	(65.4)	2,286	(15.1)	1,243	(27.1)
Service – institutional	379	(10.2)	769	(11.8)	504	(11.0)
Service – other	17	(.5)	141	(2.2)	118	(2.6)
Other non-manufacturing employment	0	(.0)	15	(.2)	13	(.3)
Manufacturing	7	(.2)	62	(1.0)	93	(2.0)
Sewing trades	666	(17.9)	1,055	(16.2)	474	(10.3)
Printing trades	11	(.3)	45	(.7)	16	(.3)
Other manufacturing	46	(1.2)	207	(3.2)	272	(5.9)
Total*	3,713	(99.9)	6,518	(100.3)	4,595	(99.9)

Source: us Census of Population, 1880, Schedule no. 1: Boston, Suffolk County, Massachusetts, in us National Archives and Records Service, *Tenth Census of the United States, 1880* (Washington: NARS, 1960), reels 552–62; us Census of Population, 1910, Schedule no. 1: Boston, Suffolk County, Massachusetts, in us National Archives and Records Service, *Thirteenth Census of the United States, 1910* (Washington: NARS, 1982), reels 614–26; us Census of Population, 1920, Schedule no. 1: Boston, Suffolk County, Massachusetts, in us National Archives and Records Service, *Fourteenth Census of the United States, 1920* (Washington: NARS, 1992), reels 728–43.
* Totals do not add up to 100 per cent because figures are rounded off.

1910, 6,518 women worked in 175 different occupations. In 1920, while the number of single English-Canadian women working in Boston dropped to 4,595, the number of occupations they listed increased to 184.

Even with allowance for variant descriptions of similar work, the number of different jobs mentioned reveals how employment opportunities for women had proliferated in the half-century since Alice and Clara Peck had come to Boston in the late 1870s (see table B.1 in appendix B). In that year, single female Maritimers had pursued ninety-four different occupations, yet over two-thirds of these women had worked in some sort of domestic service. In 1910 and 1920 employment patterns of English-Canadian women looked significantly different. Table 10 offers a summary comparison of the occupations of single Maritime women in 1880 and single English-Canadian women in 1910 and 1920 grouped by job category. Although the largest category throughout the period remained domestic service, the number of single women in these jobs declined – from 2,428 Maritime women in 1880 to 1,243 English-Canadian women in 1920. The proportion of domestics to the total workforce dropped as well – from over two-thirds in 1880 to just over one-fourth in 1920. The second most common category of work in 1880, the sewing trades, experienced a similar decline in percentage of the total workforce, from 17.9 in 1880 to 10.3 in 1920.

Percentages lost from the more traditional fields of domestic service and the needle trades were absorbed by the newer occupational areas of professional, clerical, sales, and factory work, a predictable change given the structure of Boston's economy and the transformation of the female work world. Echoing patterns revealed in these statistics, Albert Kennedy, a social worker and reformer living in the city in the 1910s, described the female "Provincials" in Boston as "teachers, masseuses, hairdressers, dressmakers, and houseworkers," who had "a large share in the office and shop work in the city" and were "in demand at hotels and in restaurants."[12] In sum, the employment patterns of single, English-Canadian women in Boston mirrored those of their counterparts in Halifax and Saint John as well as those of the larger population of single working women in the New England metropolis.

Kennedy made an additional comment about the occupations of "Provincial" women in Boston as well. "The field of nursing," he wrote, "they have almost completely captured. It is said that 75 per cent of the nurses of the state ... come from the Provinces."[13] According to Susan Reverby, who has done extensive research on Boston's nurses, the figure of 75 per cent was an exaggeration. Still, among women entering nurse training between 1900 and 1939 "nearly one third ... came from the Maritimes."[14] Occupation statistics give striking evidence of this fact. In 1910, of the 855 single English-Canadian women in Boston who held professional positions, 767, or nearly 90 per cent, were trained or student nurses. In 1920, the number of trained or student nurses remained high at 731, or 85 per cent of all professionals. In both years more single English-Canadian women pursued a nursing career than worked in any other single occupation except domestic service.

Domestic service, nursing, institutional service, clerical work, factory labour, sales – these were the employment choices of most English-Canadian women, and, if Albert Kennedy's observations are accurate, of Maritime women as well. But little other than their status as "women's work" tied these jobs together. The lives of women employed in such diverse occupations were probably as varied as the jobs themselves, so there is little foundation for collective assumptions about their experiences in Boston or their motives for leaving home. Instead, it is necessary to examine in closer detail the different work worlds that female Maritimers encountered and to explore how their Boston experiences might reflect diverse, or similar, reasons for their migration to the city.

HOUSECLEANING ON SUNDAY:
THE WORLD OF THE DOMESTIC SERVANT

For over one-third of the second-generation single English-Canadian women who came to Boston – women like Jennie Peck – the nature of work was much as it had been for their mothers and aunts. They worked as servants in the homes of others, cooking, cleaning, mending, caring for children, and responding to sundry other demands of family members who expected their immediate attention virtually any time of the night or day, seven days a week. In 1910 and 1920, as in 1880, housecleaning on Sunday meant giving up one's own scarce free time for the needs of others, and, in some cases, even acting against one's personal beliefs that work on the Sabbath violated God's laws.[15] Such was the strength of the household mistress's authority, and most accepted it as part of the job.

All the old drawbacks to domestic service remained: the long hours, the lack of free time, the arbitrariness of employers' demands, even the threat of physical and sexual abuse. But all of the perceived benefits of such employment remained as well: the comfortable, sometimes elegant, working conditions; the paid room and board; and the potential for accumulation of savings. On the surface, little about domestic service had changed since the 1880s. Nevertheless, within the more immutable outlines of the work, certain aspects of household service had undergone transformations that made life as a domestic in the 1910s, and especially the 1920s, distinct from earlier times. Two important and related changes concerned the number of live-in servant positions available and the economic status of the households who did the hiring.

In the 1870s and 1880s a typical newspaper advertisement submitted by a prospective employer requested "a Protestant girl" to do "general housework" or, sometimes, "cooking and general housework."[16] In July 1910, help-wanted ads for domestic work sounded somewhat different. Mixed in with the requests for general houseworkers were listings like the following:

An experienced nursery maid wanted to care for two children; 2 years old and 9 months. References required; good wages.

A white Protestant cook wanted in a family of three. Apply at 332 Bay State Road, Boston.[17]

The following day, under the section "Situations Wanted," these advertisements appeared:

Lady's maid. Thoroughly experienced, good seamstress, would like a situation. Apply to Miss Stutt, 52 Clarendon St.

Cook and second girl. Situation wanted by two Nova Scotia Protestant girls to work together in a private family. Good references. 83 Blue Hill Avenue. Tel. Roxbury 64.

Infants' nurse. Experienced Protestant. Best of references. Address 35 Pembroke Street.[18]

Along with these listings were similar ads submitted by prospective laundresses, travelling companions, governesses, and waitresses in private families.

Certain characteristics of these advertisements – the continued preference given to Protestants, for example, or the required references – would have been familiar to a prospective domestic in 1880. Nevertheless, the variety of jobs included under the umbrella of "domestic service" and the increasing number of ads for such specific jobs were signs of changing structures in the field. In the city of Boston, live-in servants were becoming concentrated in the households of the wealthy while middle-class families were less frequently willing, or able, to pay for round-the-clock help. One early sign of this concentration was the increased percentage of female English-Canadian live-in servants in the exclusive Back Bay district of Boston. Between 1880 and 1910, during which time the Back Bay was in Ward 11, the proportion of such servants in Ward 11 increased from 21.6 per cent (519 of 2,394 Maritime-born live-in domestics) to 37.9 per cent (797 of 2,104 English-Canadian live-in domestics). In 1920, after 1916 boundary changes had moved the Back Bay into Ward 8, that new ward housed more than half (602 of 1,108) of the city's English-Canadian live-in servants.[19] David Katzman dates the decline of live-in service in America to the period around the First World War, and general employment patterns in Boston support his findings. In the 1910s the city witnessed its first decrease in the number of female servants, from 17,071 in 1910 to 12,132 in 1920.[20]

The decline of live-in service was the product of both technological and social changes in the United States. The early years of the twentieth century had witnessed the rapid extension of electricity to the households of American cities. The development of electrical appliances such as refrigerators and washing machines soon followed, reducing the hours spent on in housework and thus the demand for outside labour.[21] Moreover, the 1910s were the years of the Great Migration, the mass movement of African Americans from the South to northern cities to seek work and an escape from the brutality of Jim Crow laws.[22] Facing limited job opportunities and racial prejudice even in the North, Black families depended on the income of both husband and wife to survive. For Black women, work options were severely restricted. Passed over for employment in stores and offices, and limited even in their opportunities for factory work, African-American women had virtually no alternative but to do some form of household work, either in their own homes, as laundresses, or in the homes of their employers. The one control they could exercise over their working conditions was to refuse to live in another's household, and they were willing to accept lower wages for that right.[23] Thus, the early twentieth century witnessed the emergence of a body of day servants who constituted a cheaper alternative to the live-in maid.

For the female Maritimer seeking full-time domestic work the concentration of positions in the homes of wealthier families had several ramifications. First, it meant fewer employment opportunities, a situation observed as early as the 1890s by the YWCA's Domestic Bureau as it struggled to find placement for prospective servants in a growing buyers' market.[24] Thus, any advantage an applicant could bring with her was critical for success, and good references were especially valuable for those new to the city. Lillian Wentzel of Upper Foster Settlement, Nova Scotia, arrived with a "Certificate of Recommendation" written by the pastor of the local Baptist Church. It read: "This is to certify that Miss Lillian J. Wentzel is a young lady of good character. I have known her for three years and take much pleasure in recommending her to any one who may need her services in any way."[25] A word of support from a minister probably carried some weight when a young woman had no previous work experience in the city, and it was a way to certify that the young woman was Protestant, still an important selling point to the elites of Boston.

Probably the best way for a young Maritime woman to find a position as a servant was through contacts with family or friends already working in the city. Jennie Peck heard about employment opportunities in Boston from her two sisters who were working as domestics there. Esther Campbell, of Milton Cross, Prince Edward Island, found her position as a nanny with the help of her older sister, who also looked after children in the city. And Lillian Wentzel, the young women who had come to Boston in 1901 armed only with her pastor's recommendation, eased the way for her sister in 1905 by asking her employer if any of her acquaintances needed servants. In response, Lillian's employer, Marion Sheldon, wrote, "Mrs. Wood is now without a girl and wants one as soon as may be, but I think she will wait for your sister for she is pleased with the idea of having a Protestant girl."[26] In a world of diminishing opportunities, compounded by new competition from Swedish immigrants, who were also Protestant and usually spoke English, having a friend or relative in Boston with contacts among the households with servants made the search for work far easier.[27] A younger sister could stay at home working or helping with family chores until an older sibling could find work for her, preventing the possibility of being unemployed in a large, foreign city.

Another impact on female Maritime migrants of the growing concentration of live-in service in wealthier families was the unfamiliarity of the job. In the 1870s and 1880s, when middle-class families routinely had a general "maid of all work," that work likely included cooking, cleaning, child care, mending, and other household chores familiar to young women who had done such work as daughters in their own homes or in the households of neighbouring families. But by the 1910s and 1920s, job descriptions for "lady's maid" or "parlour maid" – positions within larger household staffs – were less easily understood, and even familiar work like cooking and housecleaning sometimes included unfamiliar tasks. Connie Gillis, who was raised by her grandparents in the Cape Breton village of St Rose and came to Boston in the 1920s, recalled applying for the position of "parlourmaid waitress." She described the job as one "I knew nothing about, but I said I'd find out." Her work turned out to include taking "care of the dining-room table, the silver and waiting on table and the dishes afterward, and in and out of the dining room, serving and all that kind of thing."[28] Rena Annie MacDonald, also from a small Cape Breton community, recalled disguising the limited range of her cooking skills to a prospective employer and then secretly consulting a cookbook to prepare foods, like cauliflower, that she had never seen before.[29] Working in such unfamiliar settings presented the Maritime domestic with the potential for humiliation from not knowing some detail of household management or upper-class propriety, but it also offered the opportunity to expand her horizons. Connie Gillis was promoted from parlourmaid waitress to cook. She summed up her work with the comment "That was a good experience, I'll tell you. It taught me a lot."[30]

Working in the households of Boston's elites also meant the opportunity of living and working in comfortable, even opulent, surroundings. However, the price of living in the most fashionable areas of the city, like the town-house district of the Back Bay or the suburbs of Brookline, Newton, and Wellesley, was isolation from those sections of the city where other single Maritimers lived, worked, and played. This segregation, combined with very brief periods of free time, seriously limited a domestic's opportunity to meet and socialize with her compatriots, or any of the young single men and women who had come to work in Boston and congregated in the city's boarding- and lodging-house districts. Isolation and limited time off were sacrifices that women had always made to work as domestics. But by the early twentieth century, with the explosion of other job opportunities for single women, the contrast between their lives and those of female clerical, sales, and factory workers made domestic service seem even more constricting than in earlier decades. Under such circumstances it is perhaps surprising that over one-third of single English-Canadian women in 1910, and over one-quarter in 1920, still worked as live-in servants.

What were their motives for going into service when so many new employment options existed for them? It was not likely the ease of finding a job, since the demand for live-in servants was declining, nor knowledge of the tasks involved, which were no longer that similar to housekeeping in the rural Maritimes. The help and advice of other family members in service probably influenced the decision of some Maritime migrants to take positions as domestics, but the most likely reason was still the ability to accumulate savings. Jennie Peck and her sisters, like their aunts before them, entered service in Boston specifically to save money for help with expenses on the struggling family farm, and presumably other Maritime-born daughters worked as maids for similar reasons. Esther Campbell, who worked as a nanny for several Boston families, also came from a farm family, had a father who supplemented his farm earnings by working as a postmaster, and had two sisters and four brothers all working in Boston.[31] While her descendants do not recall whether she sent part of her savings to her family, they do recall her brothers doing so, suggesting that Campbell family members worked in the city as part of the familiar survival strategy of the family wage economy. It is likely that, when she could, she also contributed her share to the effort.[32] Although information on their fathers' occupations exists for only four other domestic servants, all four came from farming families. This additional evidence suggests that the nineteenth-century pattern of Maritime women working as servants to save money for family support continued into the twentieth century, though for a smaller proportion of the migrants.

THE CONTRADICTORY WORLD
OF THE STUDENT NURSE

In sharp contrast to young women like Jennie Peck, who continued to consider family support in their decision to seek work in Boston, were those who were employed as trained or student nurses. Women who came to New England after training in one of the seventy hospital-based nursing programs that were offered in Canada by 1909 had spent several years without receiving wages to share with their parents, and those who came to Boston for their training also sacrificed family support to pursue their own career.[33] In 1910 there were 767 of these women, and in 1920, 731. These numbers accounted for nearly one in eight of the single English-Canadian women listed as working in Boston in the 1910 census and nearly one in six of those listed in 1920 (see tables B.2 and B.3 in appendix B). The families of these women apparently could afford to do without their financial contribution, and the women themselves were willing to postpone earnings for the longer-term goal of becoming a professional.

However, for the young Maritime woman coming to Boston to train for a nursing career, entering the world of the student nurse meant confronting the incongruity between an ideal image and a harsh reality. In a 1911 letter of application to the training program at Boston City Hospital, Isabel Atkinson of Pictou, Nova Scotia, wrote, "It is my wish to become a nurse because I have so long felt a great interest in the profession and believe it is a calling of the highest character for which a women seems specially fitted." She then added, "One of my aunts is a nurse and through her experiences I have some idea of the severity of the training and the diligence and faithfulness required."[34] The choice of words such as "calling," "character," "diligence," and "faithfulness" is revealing, for couched in the euphemistic language of middle-class propriety (perhaps selected with the opinions of an admissions director in mind) was the candidate's understanding of the contradictory nature of nurse training in the early twentieth century. On the one hand was the ennobling ideal of service – specifically, that most feminine form of service, care giving – elevated to the status of profession by rigorous training in specialized skills and indoctrination in the ways of combatting disease and disorder.[35] On the other hand was the reality of the student nurses' daily lives, the reality of a "thirteen-hour day (or night), a six-day week, and a fifty-week year," during which they carried out virtually all the nursing chores of the hospital in return for room, board, and a small "allowance" of "eight to twelve dollars a month."[36] Those chores consisted of an unending round of bed making, washing and sterilizing equipment, bed-pan changing, furniture cleaning, and, in the case of one trainee from Cape Breton, even polishing brass door knobs, all in addition to the more direct forms of care giving such as comforting patients, taking temperatures, or giving shots.[37] It is no wonder that one trainee described herself and her fellow students as "high class maids."[38]

For most of the nineteenth century nursing had, in fact, been an extension of domestic service. In private families, nurses were hired on a temporary basis, without any special training, and were brought into the household to take care of a patient. Work demands varied from one situation to the next but often included cleaning, laundry, and food preparation as well as direct patient care. These untrained, or "professed," nurses were usually older women, often widows, who had developed their care-giving skills by nursing their own children and husbands.[39] Hospital nurses, meanwhile, lacked even the status of the private nurse; in Susan Reverby's words, they were "caught in a degraded job in a fearsome institution."[40] In a time when most medical care took place in the home, and hospitals largely served the destitute, women who staffed these institutions often came from the same lower classes as their charges and sometimes had been patients themselves.[41]

Under the influence of the work of Florence Nightingale in the Crimea and the experiences of female volunteers in the American Civil War, urban, upper-class reformers developed a new model of professional nursing that involved instructing young "gentlewomen" in hospitals to become either trained nurses in private families or hospital supervisors of nurse trainees. By stressing the nineteenth-century notion of feminine virtue, as expressed in altruistic service, self-discipline, and obedience to superiors, reformers and hospital administrators hoped to attract the daughters of middle-class families to this quintessentially female profession. With these goals in mind, the first hospital-based nurse-training programs opened in the 1870s, including one at Boston City Hospital in 1878.[42]

It did not take long for hospital administrators to discover that student nurses were not merely the Florence Nightingales of the future. They were also a source of cheap labour, cheaper, in fact, than the staff of untrained nurses who worked for wages. Hospitals with nursing schools soon depended on their trainees to handle the bulk of nursing work, and heads of these schools all too often used the ideals of self-sacrifice and obedience to enforce strict discipline and

Ward nurses and orderlies, Boston City Hospital, c. 1907. Two of the four student nurses (standing in the back row) came from New Brunswick. (Courtesy of the Boston City Hospital School of Nursing Collection, Department of Special Collections, Boston University)

demand that their charges carry out an unending routine of arduous chores with cheerfulness and efficiency. By the early twentieth century the role of student nurse had become that of a smiling "hospital machine."[43]

In spite of these harsh conditions, single Maritime women flocked to nurse-training programs in Boston in such numbers that fellow student nurses commented on their predominance in the city's hospitals. Describing Massachusetts General Hospital in the 1920s, one Cape Breton-born nurse declared, "the place was full of Nova Scotians."[44] In the same decade, 40 per cent of the students in the training program at Boston City Hospital were from the three Maritime provinces.[45] With so many compatriots in nursing schools it is likely that most Maritime applicants, like Isabel Atkinson, knew how gruelling the hospital regimen would be for trainees. Nevertheless, their numbers increased steadily in Boston's nursing programs throughout the first three decades of the twentieth century.[46] What was the powerful appeal of nursing that impelled so many Maritime women to endure grim working conditions for a paltry "allowance" in order to pursue this career?

Several factors contributed to the popularity of nursing for single women from Maritime families. Perhaps the most compelling was the belief that nursing was a "calling," an occupation that combined selfless service with professional status. Thus, nursing was a worthy career for young women to enter even if they came from families who still clung to the nineteenth-century middle-class conception of women as domestic, self-denying care-givers. In Reverby's words, "nursing seemingly offered both a livelihood and a state of grace."[47] Complementing this image of selflessness and worthiness was the model of the ideal trainee held by nursing school directors: that of a physically strong, hard-working girl who nevertheless was deferential and responsive to the efforts of her supervisors to mould her into an obedient, self-sacrificing, and refined young woman. Even in the earliest years of the program the directors of the Boston City Hospital School of Nursing made these preferences explicit on their application form: "The work of nursing demands intelligence, good temper, cleanly and orderly habits, thorough trustworthiness, and a willing spirit. No one should enter this work except from a strong sense of duty and a readiness to conform to the strict rules of discipline. It is essential that the candidate should be of unblemished character and in sound health of body and mind."[48] From the time of Florence Nightingale to the 1920s the belief persisted that the best place to find such girls was in rural families. Raised with a sense of responsibility to family needs, accustomed to hard work, and untouched by the temptations or comforts of the big city, rural daughters were considered the perfect candidates for nursing.[49]

As the twentieth century progressed, the pool of native-born rural daughters declined, particularly in New England, where many families had left barren hill farms for better opportunities in cities or further west.[50] In response, nursing schools began actively seeking country-born women from outside the immediate area, and the Maritime provinces, bordering New England, were obvious places to canvas. As far back as 1899 the Business Agency of the YWCA had played a role in placing young Maritime immigrants in nurse-training programs, but by the 1910s and 1920s the hospitals themselves were handling the recruitment and the applications of prospective trainees.[51] In the 1920s some nursing schools began placing advertisements in Maritime newspapers to publicize their programs. McLean Hospital Training School for Nurses ran neat, black-bordered ads in the Halifax *Herald* each Saturday during the autumn and winter in the mid-1920s, one of which inspired Anita Saunders Campbell to apply to its program.[52] Less-wealthy programs in smaller hospitals placed their announcements in the want-ad section, such as the one submitted by the Hart Hospital of Boston:

GIRLS WANTED: Hospital of 75 beds specializing in surgery and obstetrics, affiliated with the Bellevue Allied and Worcester State Hospitals, having an accredited training school and recognized by the American College of Surgeons, wants healthy, educated, ambitious girls to enter its approved training school for nurses. Apply The Hart Private Hospital, 95 Moreland Street, Boston 19, Massachusetts.[53]

Other hospitals depended simply on word-of-mouth advertising as more and more young Maritime women entered training programs and returned home to tell sisters and friends.

However they may have learned about nursing schools, these women shared one common trait that separated them from the majority of female Maritimers in Boston. The fact that they were attracted to a profession rooted in middle-class beliefs about appropriate female roles – and could afford to postpone decent wages to pursue that profession – suggests that, for the most part, they came from more prosperous families than those of other migrants. Although there is no reliable way of verifying it with statistics, existing descriptive evidence supports this hypothesis. Anita Saunders's father owned a jewellery business, had apple orchards, and was the local optometrist in Middleton, Nova Scotia. Although she did work as a telephone operator after high school to save money to go into training, Anita had no financial responsibilities to her family to keep her from considering a nursing career.[54] Edith Isabel Cox, who trained at Massachusetts General Hospital around the turn of the century, was the daughter of a successful merchant in Morell, Prince Edward Island.[55] And Marian Oulton, a nursing student at Boston City Hospital in 1910, came from a family in Dorchester, New Brunswick, headed by a lawyer and judge of probate.[56] Other known occupations of fathers of Maritime-born nursing students include mine manager, dairy farmer, and manager of a Western Union office. Only two nurse trainees came from an obviously working-class family: sisters Martha Ada and Ethel Marguerite Chute were the daughters of a gardener and day labourer.[57] The sacrifices involved in pursuing a nursing career apparently put it beyond the reach of many Maritime women who came to work in Boston.

Fidessa Reeves (centre, in white dress) and her family, South Freetown, Prince Edward Island, 1924. Photo taken before she returned to Boston to resume her nurse training. (Courtesy of Dr David Weale, University of Prince Edward Island, Charlettetown)

NEW OPPORTUNITIES AND FAMILIAR PROBLEMS FOR WORKING WOMEN

For those women in the 1910s and 1920s who could not afford to prepare for a career like nursing, coming to Boston meant facing the same immediate problems that had confronted an earlier generation of Maritime emigrants: finding a job and a place to live. Yet, there the similarities ended. In 1880 two out of three women had solved those problems in one stroke by finding positions as household servants; most of the rest, with limited employment options for work that paid enough for self-support, ended up working in one of the sewing trades. In the early twentieth century, prospects for young women in Boston were entirely different: jobs for women had multiplied and diversified, creating an increasingly stratified array of employment opportunities that further differentiated the work experiences of female Maritimers in Boston. Vera Marina Wotton, of Weston, Nova Scotia, and Louise Elizabeth Spidell, of Parkdale, Nova Scotia, were both employed in Boston in 1902, but their working lives had little in common. Vera worked as an office clerk in the Boston Police Department while Louise sewed shirtwaists in a local factory.[58]

In 1910 and 1920 single English-Canadian women were employed in over 160 separate occupations outside of domestic service. They were manicurists, lithographers, food canners, actresses, cigar makers, and upholsterers; they demonstrated products in department stores, aided dentists, tested electric lamps, kept accounting records, and stitched shoes. Within the broad spectrum of available employment, there were certain jobs that attracted disproportionate numbers of these women. Three such occupations were clerical work, the sewing trades, and waitressing, positions that, by their very distinctiveness, demonstrate just how diverse the work world in Boston had become for single female Maritimers. (See tables B.2 and B.3 in appendix B.)

Vera Marina Wotton came to Boston from Nova Scotia in the first decade of the twentieth century; with a high school diploma and a year of business college behind her, she joined the rapidly growing ranks of female office workers in the city. The expansion of corporations across North America, coupled with the segmentation of work in these companies, had led to an explosion in demand for all types of clerical workers, and by the early twentieth century most of these workers were women. The reasons for the feminization of office work, described earlier in the context of employment in Maritimes cities, were identical in Boston: the removal of clerical jobs from the corporate ladder and their re-creation as lower-paying, dead-end work; the surplus of young, literate women seeking work in urban settings; and the preference of employers for women who accepted lower wages and were considered more compliant and neater than men.[59] In a major metropolis like Boston the growth of private enterprises was accompanied by the expansion of municipal government agencies. One small cog in the wheel of Boston's government bureaucracy was Vera Wotton's clerk position at the police department.

Clerical work, whether stenography, typewriting, filing, or bookkeeping, shared common traits that made the work particularly appealing to the young single working woman. One obvious attraction was its wages, which, according to a 1910 study of women's earnings in Boston, provided a higher net annual income than any other non-professional work.[60] Other benefits were the clean, comfortable work setting, the steadiness of the work (in contrast to the seasonal nature of some factory work), and the perception among working women that clerical work carried a higher status than most

Stenographers in a Boston office, c. 1915 (Courtesy of the Boston Public Library, Print Department. Photograph by E.E. Bond)

occupations available to them. It even offered limited options for advancement from one position to another within a company or from a small office to a larger, more prestigious one.[61] Vera Wotton made such a move only one year after arriving in Boston, leaving her position at the police department for a clerk job in the Lowell Packing and Provision Company.

There was a serious limitation to clerical work, however: many positions required specialized training either from high school business courses or from a business college.[62] Since few high schools in the Maritime provinces were large enough to offer a thorough business curriculum, entering the world of office work meant spending part of one's earnings to take evening courses or going without wages while attending a business college. Vera Wotton, whose father owned a "moderately successful" farm in the fertile Annapolis Valley, was able to depend on parental support while she finished high school and one year of business college, apparently without jeopardizing the family's finances.[63]

It is unlikely that Louise Elizabeth Spidell's family could have afforded to make a similar sacrifice for her to train for a clerical position. She, too, grew up on a farm, but it was a subsistence farm deep in the interior of Lunenburg County, Nova Scotia, a region of rocky soil and poor drainage. On the farm the family "raised sheep for the wool to knit caps, scarfs, sox, mittens, for the long cold winter" and "grew most of their foods."[64] According to the recollections of Louise's daughter, "there was very little money" in her mother's family "to buy shoes, dresses, etc. ... in summer the children went barefoot and wore their one pair of shoes on Sunday to church."[65] Louise's daughter did not state the reason for her mother's migration to Boston but did describe her job there: a dressmaker in a shirtwaist factory. Just as Louise's background resembled that of many Maritime women from an earlier generation, so did the work she found.

In 1880 the sewing trades had been by far the most common type of employment for those single Maritime-born women who did not go into service. By 1910, although the percentage of women in household service had declined dramatically, the percentage of English-Canadian women in some form of sewing work had declined far less steeply, dropping from 17.9 per cent in 1880 to 16.2 per cent. By 1920 the proportion had decreased more significantly, but remained over 10 per cent of Boston's single English-Canadian female workforce (see Table 10). In many ways the nature of the work had not changed much either; if anything, working conditions had deteriorated over the years. Workers' wages were still based on the number of garments sewn, which placed constant pressure on them to work at a feverish pace. The workload was still tied to seasonal demand, creating peak and "dull" periods with attendant layoffs. And factory settings were often, in the words of one observer, "cramped and extremely confining."[66] Furthermore, there was constant pressure on factory owners to maintain low wages and not upgrade working conditions, because the influx of desperately poor immigrants from southern and eastern Europe in the 1890s and 1900s had led to increased competition from tenement sweatshops set up in the poorest wards of the city. There, families and boarders, squeezed into tiny rooms, stitched together pre-cut garment pieces for rates that could undercut those paid to factory workers.[67] By the 1910s union organizing and strike activity in some plants had brought improved conditions in several of Boston's shirtwaist factories but, overall, garment manufacturing remained arduous and poorly paid work.[68]

Nevertheless, for Louise Spidell and other single Maritime women from cash-poor families, the needle trades offered several advantages. First, jobs were plentiful and easy to find when one arrived in the city.[69] Second, the work required no specialized skills besides sewing techniques, which daughters on subsistence farms likely had learned at home. With minimal training on machinery a woman could begin earning wages quickly, no small consideration for new arrivals without family support. Judging from the over 1,000 single English-Canadian women who worked in the sewing trades in 1910, one can assume that many of Boston's Maritime emigrants fit that category. Given the depressed wages in the industry, it is likely that few, if any, could save money to send to families at home. Instead, like their counterparts from an earlier generation, they helped their struggling families simply by leaving home and becoming self-supporting.

Office work and factory work, then, represented the opposite ends of the spectrum of non-professional, non-live-in job opportunities for Maritime women who came to Boston. The former offered good wages and clean working conditions to those who were educated and specially trained; the latter offered little more than easy access to those who arrived without skills and needed work right away. Between these two poles was an array of other occupations, many of which had not existed in 1880. While often demanding and low-paying, these jobs presented the young female migrant with options for working outside a factory or a household setting. Two of the most popular new work settings were the department store, where young women were hired for sales work, product demonstration, and cashier jobs, and service institutions like hotels and restaurants, where, in addition to maid service, they could find work preparing food, checking hats and coats, doing laundry, and waiting tables. Of all these jobs, the one that attracted the largest number of single English-Canadian women – 421 in 1910 and 270 in 1920 – was waitressing.[70]

Like office and sales work, the field of table service throughout much of the nineteenth century had been a male preserve. Until the late 1800s most of those who dined out had been of two types: the well-to-do, who expected genteel service from a trained male staff, and working-class men, who often took meals with their pints of beer at the local saloon, an institution considered too unsavoury for women's employment.[71] Then, towards the end of the nineteenth century, single men and women began flocking to cities across North America, and boarding houses and hotels of all descriptions sprang up to house and feed them. As the twentieth century progressed, the lodging house, which did not include meals on the premises, emerged as a new form of housing. In response to an obvious need, small restaurants and dining rooms, offering inexpensive meals, opened up in lodging-house districts. All these institutions, from residential hotels to lunch rooms, served primarily the throngs of single working people. They operated on tight budgets, and soon found what department stores and offices had discovered: that they could hire women to do the same work as men and pay them lower wages.[72]

Waitressing was hard work, carried out under crowded and often dingy conditions; in Boston dining rooms that served rooming-house residents were frequently located in converted basements of lodging houses.[73] Hours of work were long – usually ten to eleven hours a day, with seven-day weeks common before the First World War and six-day weeks the rule throughout the 1920s. Moreover, because hotels and boarding houses provided their waitresses with room and board, and restaurants provided them with meals, wages were some of the lowest available to single working women. And the cost of any damages incurred by a server was deducted from her already paltry earnings.[74]

To date, there is no available information on the backgrounds of Maritime-born waitresses in Boston, so it is impossible to ascertain either their relationships to families back home or their motives for leaving. However, they represent a sizeable body of migrants who came to Boston and took jobs in the expanding service sector of the city's economy, jobs that were not available to earlier migrants. Their experiences were unique to the second generation of female Maritimers, so some speculation about why they ended up working in hotels, boarding houses, and restaurants is worthwhile.

One clue to the appeal of such work was its location. In 1910 over half of the English-Canadian waitresses – 227 of the 421 waitresses employed in hotels, restaurants, and saloons – lived in Wards 9, 10, and 12, which included Boston's South End, the major boarding- and lodging-house district. In 1920, 185 of the 270 waitresses lived in Wards 6, 7, and 8, the wards that included the South End after the city redrew its ward boundaries in 1916.[75] (For maps of Boston's ward divisions in 1910 and 1920, see figures 4 and 5.) Aside from having their meals and, in some cases, their board provided, waitresses usually lived near their place of work, which reduced commuting costs. Furthermore, in sharp contrast to those domestics isolated in the Brahman households of the Back Bay, they lived and worked surrounded by others like themselves – young, single working men and women. Perhaps their proximity to associates and the social life of the district helped to compensate for gruelling hours and low wages.

Those Maritimers who waited tables in Boston's South End lived a short distance from their compatriots in domestic service, yet their working lives were a world apart. Furthermore, a brief glimpse into the experiences of student nurses such as Anita Campbell, clerical workers such as Vera Wotton, and garment workers such as Louise Spidell reveals just how little these women's experiences had in common, other than hard work and wages below those of men with similar abilities. Each job had its own advantages and disadvantages and appealed to young women from different economic strata, a fact that undermines the idea that single Maritime women migrants in 1910 had similar backgrounds and shared common goals when working in Boston. The uneven impact of industrial capitalist development on different sectors and regions of the Maritimes had, by the early decades of the twentieth century, increased the economic distance between families in the three provinces. As a result some parents could afford to support a daughter's pursuit of specialized training for a better-paying career, some still preserved the family economy with help from a daughter's savings, and others were so poor that daughters helped simply by leaving home, without skills or support, to fend for themselves.

Thus, in spite of enormous growth in employment opportunities for women in early-twentieth-century Boston, an emigrant's choice of work was still often influenced by her family's economic status. On the other hand, there is evidence that family income did not always define a single Maritime woman's occupation. The notion, however speculative, that waitresses in lodging-house districts might have considered factors other than wages and working conditions in choosing employment is a provocative one. It introduces the possibility that motives for leaving home, once so inexorably tied to economic conditions and to a daughter's unique relationship to the family economy, might in some measure have become detached from family responsibility. Perhaps these women had other reasons for coming to Boston as well, reasons that were more similar than their varied work experiences might suggest. To explore this idea, and perhaps to uncover common experiences, it is necessary to move outside the walls of factories, offices, homes, and institutions, to examine life beyond the workplace.

5 Living in Boston in the Early Twentieth Century

Scattered across the city, working in over 170 different occupations, with goals that ranged from professional advancement to mere survival, members of the second generation of single Maritime women in Boston were a far more diverse group than those who had preceded them to the city in the late nineteenth century. Little seemed to tie their lives together besides the shared experience of leaving home and coming to a place unlike any they had known. Family need had brought many of the earlier generation to Boston, and the experience of living as servants or boarders in the homes of other families likely helped shield them from the unfamiliarity of an urban environment and the novelty of emigration as single women. By the 1910s and 1920s the size, pace, and ethnic diversity of Boston sharpened the contrast between it and the Maritimes; even years spent in the cities of the region could not fully prepare twentieth-century migrants for life in Boston. Once there, they confronted an array of different challenges, depending on the employment and housing they found. In spite of their diversity, however, two factors united them: the influence of an earlier group of migrants on their lives, and the experience of living in a twentieth-century city with throngs of other single men and women.

THE LEGACY OF THE FIRST GENERATION

Boston may have been bigger and busier in the 1910s and 1920s than in the 1880s, but for many young Maritime women, going to work there no longer seemed such a daunting prospect. The first generation of female migrants to the city had broken the mould of earlier social practice by leaving their families and going – often alone – to seek employment in a foreign metropolis. Once having deviated from this convention they had set a precedent by demonstrating to their parents and themselves that they could be self-supporting and even help with family expenses. Economic necessity had been the reason for social acceptance of a daughter's leaving home, but it was the experience that altered the way the women themselves viewed out-migration. Some apparently gained so much confidence and knowledge from their years in Boston that, as adults, they may have directly influenced the decisions of the next generation of single women to go to work there, not necessarily as a means of family support but for personal benefit.

"My mother worked in Boston before ... when she was a young girl," commented Mary Monroe Hart, who herself went to the Boston area to become a domestic servant in the early twentieth century. "And my mother always said she thought that every young girl should go to the States to find out how other people lived and how they did things."[1] How typical was that sentiment? How many young women in the 1910s and 1920s were actively encouraged to go to Boston by mothers, aunts, or other relatives and friends? Some fragments of information from other migrants and their descendants do reinforce Mary Hart's experience of family support. For example, a great-nephew of Vera Wotton, the young woman who worked in the Boston Police Department in the 1920s, suggested that Vera was told about employment opportunities in the city by her Aunt Priscilla, who herself had gone to work in Boston as a young woman and had married and then settled there.[2] Ethel Marguerite Chute, who entered a nurse-training program in Boston, first heard about the city and its possibilities for young women from her Aunts Alice and Bertha, according to her nephew Carroll Snell.[3]

Women from an earlier generation offered other benefits to twentieth-century migrants besides encouragement to move to the city or suggestions for employment. Once a young woman was in Boston, older relatives and acquaintances in the city sometimes provided her with a place to turn when problems occurred or loneliness became unbearable. When she first arrived in the Boston area and was homesick, Anita Saunders, a nurse trainee at McLean Hospital in the 1920s, turned to an old Sunday school teacher who had preceded her to the city. "I would call her when I'd get down ... and she'd come over and talk with me," Anita reported. "And she said, 'You know, Anita, I don't want you to go back home.' I said, 'I don't want to go back home, but ... I'm missing everybody so.'"[4]

The most important contribution of the first generation of female emigrants was not the direct support they offered but the example of independence they provided. The pattern of a daughter's leaving home, earning her own wages, and making her own way in a large, foreign metropolis came to be accepted by Maritime families as normal. By the twentieth century it was no longer "news" when a single woman went to Boston; it had become "the thing to do."[5] In the process the connection between out-migration and family need became blurred, and a daughter's own desire for adventure and an independent income became acceptable motives for leaving home.

The transformation of out-migration from obligation to opportunity was not lost on young women growing up in the Maritimes in the early 1900s. The pull of the big city grew until, according to one descendant of a migrant, "stories came back from Boston as an Eldorado for Maritime girls."[6] In the words of another young woman, who was herself a migrant to the city, "Everybody, everybody went, every, every, everybody went to the States."[7]

The temptation finally got so strong that those who did not leave home began to feel left out. David Weale, whose program *Them Times* on the CBC radio station in Charlottetown documented rural life and values on Prince Edward Island, described this feeling in a segment he entitled "Stuck Home": "By the time you were fourteen or fifteen years of age Boston began to act as a powerful magnet on you. Going to Boston became a rite of passage into adulthood."[8] In researching his subject, Weale gathered quotations by both men and women from the Island that reveal similar expectations among the youth of the region. One example was the commentary of a Mrs Ross, who remarked, "I felt obliged to stay on the farm and help my father. My two brothers were away at war [the First World War], and I was the only one of the sisters who was capable and strong enough to work the hundred acre farm."[9] Her use of the word "obliged" is telling. It suggests that, while responsibility for family needs had impelled an earlier generation of Maritime daughters to leave the farm, in the early twentieth century it was family obligation that kept this daughter at home.

The second generation of single Maritime women migrants owed much to their pioneering predecessors: encouragement, support, and ultimately a new societal perspective on the very purpose of out-migration. However, it would be misleading to credit all the differences in the Boston experience for the two generations to pathbreaking by the first arrivals. The city itself played a major role in transforming the migration experience: Boston in the early twentieth century had become a Mecca for single working women, who, in turn, influenced the development of institutions that were both liberating and supportive.

NEW FREEDOM IN BOSTON:
INDEPENDENT LIVING

Lucille Eaves, a researcher for the Women's Educational and Industrial Union, reported in 1917 that among the eight largest cities in the
United States, Boston had the greatest proportion of single, working
women living as boarders. Believing this situation to be unprecedented, she added that "the lone woman of our great cities presents
a new phase of social evolution."[10] With 33,697 Maritimers living in
Boston in 1915, it seems unlikely that a large number of single
women from the region would have fit Eaves's description of a "lone
woman."[11] Many of the second-generation migrants probably had
older relatives who resided in the city and could provide them a
place to live. Was this, in fact, the living arrangement commonly
followed?

Mary McSwain, who came to Boston in 1916, reported that she
decided to go to the city to do clerical work because she had three
aunts there who took her in. She continued to live with them during
her entire stay in Boston while she first took business courses and
then worked as a stenographer for several institutions.[12] However,
figures in table 11 indicate that Mary McSwain's decision to move in
with older relatives was atypical. In 1910 only 178, or 2.4 per cent, of
the single English-Canadian women living in Boston chose to live
with their aunts; in 1920 the number had dropped to 116, or 2.2 per
cent. Instead, these women preferred to reside with relatives of their
own generation (sisters and brothers) or on their own. While not all
fit the category of the "lone women" of Eaves's description, these
migrants were not living under the authority of an elder.

This preference among twentieth-century migrants for living with
their peers becomes even more apparent when their housing patterns are compared with those of the 1880 cohort. The most obvious
difference across the three sets of figures is the rapid decline in the
percentage of women who lived as servants – from 64.9 per cent in
1880 to 24.3 per cent in 1920. This decrease is simply another measure of the declining popularity of live-in domestic service as
employment for second-generation migrants. The percentage of
these women who lived with aunts remained roughly the same, at
between 2.0 and 2.4 per cent, as did the percentage who boarded in
private families, between 12.9 and 13.7 per cent. Thus the 50 per cent
of single women who had moved out of the category of live-in servant in the years from 1880 to 1920 were not housed with other
families either. Instead, the declining percentage of live-in servants
was replaced by increases in the percentage of women housed by

Table 11
Relationship to head of household of single Maritime women, 1880, and single
English-Canadian women, 1910 and 1920, Boston

Relationship to head of household	1880		1910		1920	
	No.	(%)	No.	(%)	No.	(%)
Head	126	(3.0)	694	(9.5)	714	(13.6)
Sister	187	(4.5)	558	(7.6)	544	(10.3)
Sister-in-law	123	(3.0)	402	(5.5)	295	(5.6)
Niece	85	(2.0)	178	(2.4)	116	(2.2)
Aunt, cousin, other relative	30	(0.7)	120	(1.6)	104	(2.0)
Boarder, private home	543	(13.1)	946	(12.9)	721	(13.7)
Boarder, boarding/lodging house	366	(8.9)	2,058	(28.1)	1,487	(28.2)
Servant	2,697	(64.9)	2,365	(32.3)	1,281	(24.3)
Total*	4,157	(100.1)	7,321	(99.9)	5,262	(99.9)

Source: US Census of Population, 1880, Schedule no. 1: Boston, Suffolk County, Massachusetts, in US National Archives and Records Service, *Tenth Census of the United States, 1880* (Washington: NARS, 1960), reels 552–62; US Census of Population, 1910, Schedule no. 1: Boston, Suffolk County, Massachusetts, in US National Archives and Records Service, *Thirteenth Census of the United States, 1910* (Washington: NARS, 1982), reels 614–26; US Census of Population, 1920, Schedule no. 1: Boston, Suffolk County, Massachusetts, in US National Archives and Records, *Fourteenth Census of the United States, 1920* (Washington: NARS, 1992), reels 728–43.

* Totals do not add up to 100 per cent because percentages are rounded off

themselves, with same-generation relatives, and especially in boarding and lodging houses.

In the 1910 and 1920 censuses, single English-Canadian women used the terms "boarder," "lodger," and "roomer" interchangeably to describe the condition of living in a house divided into individual rooms for rent. In this study, all those designations have been included under the single category of "boarder," the term used by first-generation Maritime migrants when they lived in such divided housing. This categorization masked a fundamental transformation in the nature of housing for single men and women that had taken place in the years between 1880 and the 1910s: the virtual disappearance of the true boarding house and its replacement with the lodging, or rooming house.

In 1913 a Harvard economist, Albert Benedict Wolfe, published a study of residential patterns entitled *The Lodging-House Problem in Boston*. A work of over 200 pages, it recorded in careful detail the evolution of a new form of housing designed specifically to serve single men and women who, by choice or necessity, lived apart from their families.[13] Throughout most of the nineteenth century such unattached individuals had boarded either with families or in the traditional boarding house. In both places, rent included at least two meals, which were usually eaten with others in the household. Boarders also had to observe the rules of the premises, such as restrictions on visits by the opposite sex to supervised meetings in the parlour.[14] Wolfe described the "old-time" boarding house as having "something of the home element" about it, with landladies who took a "personal interest" in their boarders and residents who "often found themselves becoming a part of the family even against their wills."[15]

The lodging house had little in common with these paternalistic institutions. Located in older neighbourhoods with declining real estate values, lodging houses were the creation of real estate specu-lators who purchased single-family dwellings, renovated them, and then ran them as a business, gleaning as much income from each building as possible. All available space was divided into rental units. The dining rooms of the old boarding houses were sacrificed for extra rooms to let, so lodgers were left to take their meals in the restaurants and cafés that sprang up nearby. Over time, as more older dwellings were converted into these rooming houses and more eating establishments opened up to serve their occupants, whole neighbourhoods were transformed into enclaves of housing for single residents. In Boston the largest of these districts was located in the old South End, which in 1910 encompassed the northern edge of Ward 9 and most of Ward 12 and in 1920 included Ward 6, the southern end of Ward 7, and parts of Wards 12 and 13 (see figures 4 and 5).[16]

The lodging-house keeper was almost invariably a woman, often divorced or widowed, who purchased the furniture and rights to charge rents but not the building itself. Her entire livelihood was derived from what the lodgers paid her; from that she was required to pay coal, gas, water, laundry, and maintenance costs as well as her own rent to the building owner. Under such stringent economic con-ditions, it is not surprising that the lodging-house keeper was more concerned with keeping her rooms filled than with monitoring the behaviour of her tenants.[17]

As a result, lodging-house life was virtually unregulated. Men and women from varied backgrounds lived under the same roof with little restriction on their activities so long as they paid their rent on time. There were no supervised parlours for entertaining guests; like the dining rooms of older boarding houses, they had been turned into rooms to let. Some lodging-house keepers did

Row houses in Boston's South End; typical buildings converted to lodging houses in the 1900s and 1910s. (Author's photo)

forbid their boarders to have members of the opposite sex in their rooms, but others did not, and few had the time or the motivation to enforce such rules. According to Wolfe, in certain areas the line soon blurred between "disreputable" lodging houses and houses of prostitution.[18]

But the image of lodging houses as dens of iniquity was in large part a distortion, the creation of a middle-class mentality worried about a new generation of young people, particularly young women, living outside the social controls of a family. As Lucille Eaves noted with undisguised concern, "large numbers of virtuous women from whom the mothers of future generations may be drawn have never before been found living independently outside of family groups."[19] In fact, the residents of most lodging houses were the same young men and women who worked in the offices, behind the sales counters, and in the restaurants, hotels, and even the factories of Boston. They struggled to afford rent and meals (costing at least $5.00 per week in 1913) and spent many evenings washing and repairing their clothes so that they could live in "an unheated and stuffy side room" or "share a poorly furnished and often untidy square room with some roommate."[20] It was a high price to pay to live independently, but apparently it was worth it. According to Wolfe, the lodging house emerged as the preferred form of housing for single working people "as a natural result of new conditions," in particular "the rising demand, on the part of boarders, for more freedom and a bohemian existence."[21]

Among these lodgers were 2,058 single English-Canadian women in 1910 and 1,487 in 1920 (see table 11). They represented over one-quarter of unmarried English-Canadian women living in Boston and over one-third of those who were not live-in servants. While these figures include women such as student nurses who lived in more closely supervised settings, many Maritime migrants were among the masses of lodging-house dwellers. Contemporary observers made special mention of Canadians, most of whom were Maritimers, living in lodging houses. Robert A. Woods, a social worker who wrote about Boston's lodging houses in 1898, noted that most of the "British Americans" living in such quarters were from Nova Scotia, with New Brunswick in second place.[22] In 1913 Wolfe reported that "the Canadians" in lodging houses "come mostly from the Lower Provinces" and added that the young women among them "who are not household servants are manicurists, dressmakers, waitresses and the like." He also commented that they "always have hosts of cousins and other relatives scattered about in the lodging-houses," so living independent of one's family did not necessarily mean struggling alone in an unfamiliar or threatening place.[23]

In fact, contrary to the picture of lodging-house life depicted by social critics – a dreary image of isolation and loneliness – lodgers created their own lively, peer-based subculture around the very facilities built to serve their special needs.[24] The most common such institution was the basement dining room, another space carved out of the lodging house to increase profits for the real estate speculator. Here, lodgers purchased meal tickets for various combinations of breakfasts, lunches, and dinners, which might include "soup, a choice of beef or mutton, boiled potatoes, 'side beans,' stewed corn, and blueberry pie, with tea or coffee."[25] The dining rooms and cafés also provided informal settings for making new acquaintances or meeting old friends away from the watchful eyes of elders.

Eating establishments were not the only facilities in Boston's South End that catered to the interests of lodging-house residents. Along the major thoroughfares of the South End there were saloons and pool halls, dance halls and theatres.[26] Taken together, these enterprises made up the inexpensive entertainment that historian Kathy Peiss has labelled "cheap amusements."[27] Like the lodging house and the basement dining room, they flourished because they satisfied the demands of a new generation of single working men and women who wanted to spend their free time at play with their peers.

The bars attracted a largely male clientele, although two of the single Canadian women working in Boston claimed to be waitresses in saloons, and some of the other table workers may have worked in establishments that served liquor. Pool halls in Boston's South End were also male preserves. Another establishment that served alcohol was the beer garden, at least one of which operated through the summer "in the district of poorer and 'shadier' lodging-house streets." According to Wolfe, men and women met there for "assignation, openly or secretly."[28] Whether this assessment of the beer garden was the biased view of a social reformer or an accurate depiction, the beer garden was a visible symbol that the South End did provide places where men and women could meet privately. Prostitution was also a reality in the district.[29]

Dance halls also served as settings for social and sexual encounters among lodgers and other working-class youth, and they drew their share of criticism from reformers of the day. "The public dance-hall is everywhere believed to be a source of evil, and at best radically in need of regulation," wrote two settlement workers from the South End in yet another study of young working women in Boston. While conceding that dancing offered healthy recreation, and the brightly lit surroundings a welcome change from the dreariness of monotonous work, these critics bemoaned the lack of supervision and the "dangerously prevalent indecent dances" that characterized the halls.[30] Whatever their image among reformers, they were undeniably popular. Wolfe observed that dances lasted from 8 PM to 2 AM, and "it is not uncommon for young men and women to dance these hours nearly every night and work all day."[31]

Less overtly sexual but still problematic to middle-class commentators were the four theatres in the South End that offered inexpensive live entertainment in the form of vaudeville acts or melodrama.[32] To the critics such places provided nothing but "sensationalism and sentimentalism" similar to the "cheap unreal novel," but to the young women who attended performances they simply offered pleasant diversions.[33] Like the dance halls, the theatres thrived in the face of reformers' complaints because they satisfied the demand for low-cost entertainment especially among single working women who, for the first time, had a bit of money to spend and the desire, and freedom, to spend it on themselves. In the 1910s and 1920s it was the new technology of motion pictures, not middle-class opprobrium, that threatened the comedies and romances of live theatre.

The "cheap amusements" in Boston's South End were concentrated on major thoroughfares like Washington and Northampton Streets, which were also public transportation routes. Thus, they were easily accessible to those living outside the lodging-house district as well as South End residents. But not all female Maritimers in Boston were part of this new subculture. For some second-generation migrants older patterns of social life persisted. Lulu Pearl Dempsey, who came to Boston in 1914, lived in a boarding house owned by her cousins. According to the recollections of her grandson, her social life centred around the friends and relatives from Stonehaven, New Brunswick, who gathered there.[34] Jennie Peck, who migrated in the 1920s, was as devout a member of the Roxbury Adventist Church as her aunts Clara and Alice had been in the 1880s. It is unlikely that she would have considered going to a dance hall. While working as a domestic she spent her few hours of spare time with her sister and other relatives in the city.[35]

Even for Maritime women in more restricted environments, Boston in the 1910s and 1920s offered opportunities that earlier migrants had not had. Jennie Peck spent her Sunday afternoons on excursions with her sister. Using the city's extensive public transportation system, they travelled to various sights in the area. In the spring they visited the Arnold Arboretum to see the lilacs in bloom. And in the summer they would head for the beach.

In early-twentieth-century Boston, going to the beach usually meant going to either Revere or Nantasket Beach, and going to either meant far more than sun, sand, and waves. In the first decade of the century, entrepreneurs, capitalizing on the growing popular interest in commercialized leisure activities, built large amusement parks at each venue, complete with roller coasters, Wild West shows, and tunnels of love. By the 1920s the large parks had folded, but many of the amusements – the concession stands, the game booths, even some of the rides – continued to attract a diverse group of mostly working-class locals.[36] Jennie Peck, proper and religious, described the crowds at Revere Beach as "riff raff," and Helen Ross, a migrant from Tusket, Nova Scotia, commented that the area was a prime stalking ground for white slavers, one of whom attempted to seduce her sister.[37] However, such dangers did not prevent either of these women from going there for an afternoon's entertainment.

Eva Aulenback, from Blockhouse, Nova Scotia, came to the Boston area in the 1920s and worked in a hat factory. In the evening she wrote down a few words about her day in her diary. Here she describes a social life that encompassed the range of possible activities that were available to a single Maritime woman in the early twentieth century. Some entries depict a life similar to that of migrants from an earlier time: after work she visited with friends, took walks, and occasionally cared for another family's baby. In July she returned home to Blockhouse, where she visited relatives and attended the local Baptist church. Other entries, however, describe events such as attendance at movies and dances, and trips to

Norwood, to Foxboro, to Framingham "alone by bus," to Boston for shopping and to see the Franklin Park Zoo. On different occasions she also "rode" with one man to Medfield – in an automobile, perhaps – and spent the evening out with another man at a "Walpole lunch room."[38] These activities reveal an after-work life of striking diversity and mobility, the result of significant changes in urban life that had taken place between 1880 and 1930: the development of new forms of transportation, new types of entertainment like motion pictures, and new social values that permitted a single woman greater independence of action.

NEW FREEDOM IN BOSTON: PERSONAL AMBITION

Mixed in with the dance halls, cafés, and theaters of Boston's South End was another institution that lacked the glitter of its neighbours but served a valuable purpose for the residents of area lodging houses. In the 1910s English High School, by day a regular city school, reopened at night as Central Evening High School. According to its own advertising the school provided "special advantages for those who are employed during the day and who desire a thorough and practical training to assist them in securing advancement in business. The courses of study comprise all the studies of the day high school and of the practical business college."[39] Evening courses were free and were open to all persons over fourteen years old and living in Boston. And, according to Albert Wolfe, "a considerable share of its pupils are said to be lodgers."[40]

Freedom from parental controls did not lead automatically to dissipation for single men and women in Boston's lodging houses. Some devoted their evenings to completing high school diplomas or taking business courses that would enable them to leave table service, factory work, or sales clerking for the prestige and higher wages of office work. Such an option for upward mobility, though severely limited, was a new experience for women and a direct result of the proliferation of female occupations. Dead-end jobs in themselves, positions like stenographer, telephone operator, bookkeeper, and department-store buyer represented significant steps up from the textile mill, shoe factory, sweatshop, and servants' quarters hat had been virtually the only choices for the single woman a few decades earlier. The existence of institutions like Central Evening High School provided ways for even poorer working women to train for a better job.

It is impossible to know how many female Maritimers were students at schools like Central Evening High School, but Jennie Peck was among them. A domestic servant who still sent money home to help her family, she nevertheless used a portion of her scant free time to attend Burdett College for business courses. She was rewarded for her efforts almost immediately when the head of the household where she worked offered her a new position at his business, a tool-making company.

Mary McSwain, who came from a prosperous family, had already attended a year of business college in Charlottetown before she left Prince Edward Island. When she arrived in Boston she enrolled in additional business classes that enabled her to find work as a stenographer in a downtown office.[41] Lulu Pearl Dempsey, one of nine children from a small farm in northern New Brunswick, did not arrive in the city with either the financial cushion or the educational background of Mary McSwain. She was employed in a chocolate factory, yet she, too, took advantage of educational opportunities in the city by attending high school classes at night. These female migrants evidently considered self-improvement, whether occupational or educational, a valuable part of their stay in Boston.

There is also evidence that some women planned their occupational mobility while in the Maritimes and came to Boston to pursue a better-paying, more prestigious position. Anita Saunders and two other female friends were working as telephone operators in Middleton, Nova Scotia, when they read an advertisement for McLean Hospital's nursing program in the local paper. One night at work they decided that they would all save their money and go to Boston to train.[42] Apparently, they were far from unique in making the move from the switchboard to the hospital corridor. The *Monthly Bulletin*, a publication of the Maritime Telegraph and Telephone Company for its employees, included a feature entitled "District Notes," which included information about the activities of current and former operators. The following are typical of the numerous notices published in the 1910s and 1920s about employees that left to enter nursing programs:

Miss S. Burns, "A" Operator, resigned her position on the 15th of March. She left for Taunton, Mass., on the 18th where she intends studying to qualify as a nurse. We wish her every success in her new undertaking.[43]

Miss Sarah Kennedy, one of our former "A" operators, at present training in Dorchester Hospital, Mass., motored to Sydney and paid us a visit.[44]

Misses Cecelia Brown and Irene Brown are leaving on July 25th to enter
Somerville Hospital as student nurses.[45]

The corporate publishers of the *Monthly Bulletin* obviously noticed,
perhaps with dismay, the propensity of their female staff to use
employment at the telephone company as a stepping stone to a nursing career in the United States. In yet another article on a departing
employee, the author of the "Head Office" column wrote, "Another
recruit has joined the great army of nurses. One more stenographer
has abandoned 'pot hooks' in favor of thermometers."[46] This recruit
was one of ten such prospective nurses to leave the company in 1926
alone.

The progression from a Maritime telephone company to a New
England nursing school was an option reserved primarily for the
more educated, better-dressed, and more articulate single women of
the region, those whose voice and demeanour were pleasing to customers who picked up a telephone or entered a telephone office. However, the perception that the Boston States offered female occupational
mobility pervaded all levels of society. Marie LeLievre, a single Acadian woman from Cheticamp, Nova Scotia, finished two years of high
school and then worked as a housekeeper. In 1916, at age twenty-six,
she decided to go to work at the Waltham Watch Company – a popular destination for French-speaking Maritimers – because she could
earn more money there. (The attraction of a community of fellow
Acadians in Waltham, five miles west of Boston, likely influenced her
choice of destination and workplace as well.) According to her daughter, Marie LeLievre also "upgraded her schooling" while in Waltham,
most likely by taking evening courses.[47]

LeLievre worked in Waltham for eight years before returning to
Cheticamp to marry a long-time acquaintance. She had put off marriage until age thirty-four while she earned her own income, lived in
a boarding house with friends, and extended her education.[48] Many
single Maritime women who went to work in Boston postponed
marriage; nevertheless there was a difference between those earlier
migrants who had gone to fulfil a family responsibility and those
who went in the early twentieth century for their own reasons. For
example, Mary Josephine Waterman of South Brookfield, Nova
Scotia, received a proposal of marriage in the 1920s when she was
eighteen years old. According to her daughter, she did not want to
marry right away and instead chose to go to Boston to train for a
nursing career. Ill health prevented her from completing the training
program; only then did she return to South Brookfield and, a year
later, marry the man who had proposed.[49]

Contemporary witnesses noted this propensity of single Maritime women to put off marriage for the chance to live in Boston and earn their own wages. Albert Kennedy, a settlement worker in Boston, wrote about these female migrants, commenting that "their incomes are equal [to] or better than those of men whom they know, and they refuse to exchange single competence for the double poverty that must result in marriage."[50] According to Kennedy, many of these women, having enjoyed the benefits of "single competence," never married.[51] Even those who, like Marie LeLievre and Mary Josephine Waterman, eventually did wed, chose first to pursue an independent course for a time – to travel to Boston, to find work, in some cases to move to a better job or a higher education level, and to demonstrate to themselves and others a level of autonomy that those daughters who went directly from their family to marriage could not know. No wonder that one woman who had gone to the city in the 1920s reported to her son "that in her time it was considered 'that anyone that never got to Boston would die a fool.'"[52]

By the early twentieth century the lure of life – or, more accurately, a period of one's life – in the Boston area had become a powerful temptation for daughters of Maritime families. Succumbing to Boston fever was an experience that united these young women and separated them from their first-generation counterparts. Some, perhaps a majority, of these migrants went to Boston purely out of self-interest, and by placing their own concerns above those of their families they were staking out new territory of acceptable social behaviour for single women in the Maritimes.

However, when set into a larger context of changing family dynamics in late industrial capitalist societies, their behaviour appears less of a departure from the norm. Their actions were no different from those of the many other single women who migrated from the countryside to the city in early-twentieth-century North America – the so-called "women adrift," whose existence caused such alarm among social commentators such as Lucille Eaves.[53] Middle-class reformers feared for the future of parental authority, female morality, and, by extension, social order, as, given an unprecedented array of job opportunities in urban areas, young single women took up the opportunity to leave their families and strike out on their own.

Furthermore, by acting in their own self-interest these women were following the process of individuation that Louise Tilly and Joan Scott described in their discussion of working-class daughters in early-twentieth-century Europe. Although Tilly and Scott focused much of their study on daughters living at home and still contributing to the family income, they observed that these young women, more highly educated than their nineteenth-century counterparts and with a broader range of available employment, gained more control over disposition of their earnings and increasingly spent money on themselves for leisure activities and consumer goods. In this period of the "family consumer economy" daughters increasingly indulged themselves in ways that nineteenth-century daughters, most of whom were domestic servants, could not, or chose not to do.[54] By responding to the attraction of living independently in Boston – by choosing to room with their peers, to spend part of their income on the amusements in the city, and in some cases to pursue their own careers – single Maritime women in the 1910s and 1920s followed a variant pattern of the same process of individuation that Tilly and Scott described. In terms of motives for leaving home their behaviour more closely mirrored that of their contemporaries in European cities than that of their own mothers and aunts.

What this comparison ignores, however – and what, by extension, may have been overlooked in other studies of female rural-to-urban migration in the late nineteenth and early twentieth centuries – is the important role that the very mothers and aunts who had not acted independently played in paving the way for the next generation of migrants. Without doubt, the explosion of female occupations that accompanied corporate growth and work segmentation in capitalist countries created the economic conditions that allowed single women to earn their own wages and become self-supporting. But opportunity was not enough. Without a social ethic that supported, in some cases encouraged, daughters to go to the city for their own self-development, fewer daughters would have rebelled against prevailing values and left home just for their own interest. It also took the experiences of a first generation of daughters, who went to work in Boston as their contribution to the family economy but returned (or remained) with a new sense of self-confidence, to transform societal attitudes towards female migration.

Epilogue and Conclusion

The attraction of Boston, a powerful magnet for single Maritime women in the first three decades of the twentieth century, was short-lived. By the 1930s legal and economic barriers had made it extremely difficult for any Canadians to enter the United States to work. The twin forces behind the construction of these barriers were a growing anti-immigrant sentiment among native-born Americans and the high unemployment rates of the Depression years.

Anti-foreign attitudes among native-born Americans, an undercurrent running throughout the history of the United States, have tended to surface during periods of national stress. In the late nineteenth and early twentieth centuries the rapid rate of social and economic change – massive immigration, urbanization, industrial growth, and technological developments – provided such a climate.[1] A heavy influx of migrants from Asia and southern and eastern Europe in that period exacerbated nativist prejudice, and pressures mounted to limit their entry into the country. The first large-scale restriction was enacted in the late nineteenth century with the Chinese Exclusion Act of 1880. More such policies were established in the 1910s, when Congress passed legislation that increased the head tax levied on immigrants to $8.00 per person, established a literacy requirement, and excluded all Asians from entry into the country. The Emergency Quotas Act of 1921 and the Immigration Act of 1924 further narrowed the spectrum of acceptable aliens. These laws introduced the requirement that some immigrants have visas to enter the country; those visas were assigned according to a quota system based on the number of persons of that nationality already resident in the United States, a system that heavily favoured the northern European Protestant countries. While Canadians were specifically exempted from the quota system, they had to obtain a visa to remain in the country more than six months and had to pay the same $8.00 head tax. During the 1920s visas were readily available. However, once the visa system was in place the number of immigrants allowed to work in the United States came under the control of the U.S. Immigration and Naturalization Service, which had the authority to limit those numbers. Another feature of the 1924 act was the expansion of the Border Patrol and an increase in the number of patrolled crossings along the Canadian border. Although established to prevent illegal entry of migrants from quota nations, these border patrols became visible symbols of new barriers to cross-border movement.[2]

With structures in place for controlling immigration, the stage was set for further restrictions. The arrival of the Great Depression, with its unemployment rate of over 20 per cent, provided the impetus for such limitations, and by the early 1930s immigration had fallen to a record low.[3] With demand for jobs far outstripping available employment, it became extremely difficult for all foreigners, including Canadians, to obtain visas allowing them to remain in the country more than six months. Mary McSwain Hart, who came from Cape Breton to work in the Boston area in the mid-1930s, took her sister's old job of caring for the young son of a Brookline family. According to Mary, her sister returned home because "you were only allowed to stay in the country six months." When asked if it was difficult to get a work permit she responded, "Well, you weren't supposed to work. See, you were really working illegally there." After her six months, Mary went back to Nova Scotia and her sister resumed her former job as governess for another six months. The next year Mary found a family in the Boston area willing to sponsor her to take care of their daughter; only through such intervention could she legally remain in the United States for more than half a year.[4]

Legal restrictions on Canadian immigration were compounded by the lack of employment opportunities. Although women in clerical and service positions were less likely to lose their jobs during the Depression than men working in factories, few enterprises expanded during the 1930s, and those women still holding jobs were loath to give them up. Those Maritime women who had obtained visas and had steady work in fields like nursing might be able to stay, as could those women who married an American or became a naturalized citizen. Others had to leave, and very few young women migrated to

Boston to take their place. It had become almost impossible to work in New England for the period of one's youth. Instead, it was likely to be more economical for Maritimers from rural areas to return to the family farm than to struggle alone in the city. Thus, by the 1930s female migration in the Maritime provinces had come full circle. Originally forced by economic dislocations to leave the family farm and earn cash, the daughters of the region were now forced by harsh economic conditions back to the farm, where their traditional subsistence skills would be of use when cash wages were not available.

Out-migration from the Maritime provinces resumed after the end of the Second World War. While other parts of North America experienced postwar prosperity, the Maritime economy stagnated.[5] However, the destination of emigrants was no longer Boston, or any other part of the United States, where immigration restrictions on Canadians seeking work remained in place. In Canada, meanwhile, increased automobile ownership and the construction of the Trans-Canada Highway improved transportation connections between the Atlantic region and the rest of the country. The economy of central Canada expanded rapidly after the war, and the cities of the region became the new destination for both male and female Maritimers.[6] Helen Cox, of Morell, Prince Edward Island, became one of these migrants to central Canada when, in 1943, she moved to Toronto to work in the office of an airline. In choosing to leave the Maritimes and find a clerical position, she followed the example of her mother, Mary McSwain Cox, who had gone away to work in a Boston office twenty-seven years earlier. However, she did not retrace her mother's footsteps. By the 1940s the well-worn path from the Maritimes to the Boston States was gated, and access to the jobs at the other end was strictly limited.[7]

Thus, 1930 marked the end of the exodus from the Maritime provinces to the United States, a migration that included tens of thousands of single women who went to Boston in search of work in the late nineteenth and early twentieth centuries. The attitudes and behaviour of these women, as revealed in census data, in their own comments, and in the recollections of their descendants, provide insights into an aspect of this process that historians up to now have largely ignored: the experiences of female migrants, whose numbers were always comparable to, and at times greater than, those of their male counterparts. The final step in fleshing out the historical picture of out-migration is to integrate the experiences of single women and then reassess current historical interpretations of the phenomenon with new sensitivity to gender.

Up to now, the most important historical debates about Maritime out-migration have focused on what economic forces were at work in the region that caused young men and women to leave to find work. Marcus Hansen, J. Bartlet Brebner, and Alan Brookes believed that the decline of the Maritimes' traditional staples economy was the primary impetus for depopulation. Gary Burrill, echoing the structural interpretation of Henry Veltmeyer, argued that the unevenness of capitalist development in North America led inexorably to out-migration from the Maritimes because larger, more profitable enterprises from outside the region undermined indigenous industries and drove the populace away. Patricia Thornton also connected out-migration to economic underdevelopment, but she reversed cause and effect by contending that the departure of young skilled workers in itself contributed to the region's decline.

A closer look at the behaviour of the first generation of single female migrants to Boston quickly reveals the inadequacies of all these interpretations. The great majority of the women who went to the city became domestic servants. They abandoned staples production only to the extent that they no longer helped with home production, and much of what they had produced was being made in factories by the time they left. These women could not be considered to have lost wage work at home either, for those few who had worked outside the home before they went to Boston had probably earned far less from employment in a neighbour's household or taking in sewing. Finally, it is difficult to picture these rural daughters as Thornton's skilled workers whose departure led to the economic decline of the region. Though some of the women who remained in the Maritimes did end up in textile mills or lobster canneries, few of the early migrants to Boston worked in industry, and the preponderant majority of those who did ended up in garment factories or, at best, as seamstresses. It is highly unlikely that the future of the Maritime economy rested on the shoulders of a few needle workers or a large number of domestic servants.

However, if a new understanding of the experience of female migrants encourages a reassessment of the major economic interpretations of out-migration as too simplistic, it does not mean that the process was entirely independent of the economic changes that were occurring in the same period. A careful study of the behaviour and motives of the first-generation migrants to Boston has revealed a direct link between structural changes in the traditional staples economy of the region and the departure of its daughters. The connection was not employment opportunities for this generation – something that would not have factored into a daughter's decision to leave home – but strategies for survival made by rural Maritime families when capitalist development threatened their economic security. Recent research on the nineteenth-century rural family economy has demonstrated that a majority of households in the region required the paid and unpaid labour of many family members to ensure year-to-year subsistence. As industrial capitalism penetrated the region – and especially in the years after Confederation, when the Canadian government reinforced the economic connections between the Maritimes and central Canada – the rising need for cash, the increased competition from central Canadian agriculture and industry, and the growth of factory production all threatened the existence of the rural family economy. Sending daughters as well as sons out to earn wages was one strategy that these families used to preserve their farms and way of life, and the most popular destination – the closest location that offered plentiful jobs and decent wages – was the city of Boston.

Introducing gender into the complex relationship of economic change and out-migration uncovers the critical role that family strategies played in determining who left home, when, and why, particularly in the late nineteenth century. Family concerns probably affected a son's as well as a daughter's decision to go away to work. A son's autumn excursion to Manitoba to help with the wheat harvest could just as well have been a means to earn needed cash for the parental family as a source of savings for his own future. In Jennie Peck's family – a traditional subsistence-farm household that survived into the 1920s – her brothers and sisters all sent money back from Boston to help pay for farm expenses. The relationship of male out-migration to the family economy needs further exploration but also points to the importance of introducing gender analysis and family concerns into the historical debate about Maritime depopulation.

Another issue ignored in existing interpretations of out-migration and brought to light through studying the experiences of women migrants is the changing nature of the migration process from the late nineteenth to the early twentieth centuries. Up to now, out-migration has been addressed as a single phenomenon, a steady stream of youth who responded to declining economic conditions by departing from the region to find seasonal or permanent work elsewhere. However, an exploration of the lives of single women migrants to Boston over a sixty-year period has uncovered evidence that contradicts the idea of an unchanging motive for leaving home. In the nineteenth century most single women from the Maritimes probably did go to Boston as part of a family response to changes threatening traditional economic ways. Some daughters, like Jennie

Peck, continued that pattern of dutiful behaviour well into the twentieth century. But by the 1910s and 1920s the impact of late industrial
capitalism in both the Maritimes and the cities of North America had
significantly altered economic conditions for women. In a striking
irony, the very concentration of capital that undermined the smaller
indigenous enterprises of the region and led to the dominance of the
Maritime economy by outside interests also brought expanded job
opportunities for women. The growth of businesses led to the creation of new areas of office employment outside the ladder of corporate advancement, ideal work for young educated women who were
willing to work without any expectation of upward mobility. The
introduction of new technology and new product-marketing techniques led to an increase in jobs ranging from telephone operator to
sales clerk to waitress. While none of these occupations paid high
wages – and some jobs paid very little for long hours of hard work
– they did create an unprecedented opportunity for single women to
go to a city, find work, and live independently (if frugally) at least
for a time between high school and marriage.

Expanded job choices in cities from Sydney to Saint John attracted
growing numbers of single women from rural areas but did not slow
female emigration from the region. The same forces that had generated new occupations for women in Maritime cities were operating
in Boston as well, but on a massive scale. As a major service and
mercantile centre the city experienced an explosion of new jobs for
women in department stores, lunch rooms, offices, and hospitals,
and an influx of single women eager to fill these positions. By the
early years of the twentieth century Boston's population included a
large number of single men and women who lived, worked, and
played together in establishments created especially for their own
needs. Maritime daughters, who in earlier years would more likely
have lived as boarders or servants with another family, were now a
part of this independent youth culture. Moreover, their declining
numbers in the field of domestic service and their preference for
living with their peers suggest that they no longer placed family
support ahead of their own interests, preferring to spend their wages
on independent housing than to save money to send home.

Thus, in the early twentieth century the structural changes within
industrial capitalism continued to undermine the economy of the
Maritime provinces, and emigration to the Boston States continued
unabated, but for female migrants the relationship between the two
processes was different from what it had been in the nineteenth century. What had begun as a way for daughters to help preserve the
traditional family economy had increasingly become an act of self-

interest born of new opportunities for female employment and the precedent set by the earlier generation of single women whose experiences in Boston had became a part of the collective memory of the region. Mothers, aunts, and other older women had blazed the trail to New England as a means of fulfilling family obligations, but in the process some of them had also discovered a sense of autonomy that they wished their daughters to experience as well. Their support likely helped perpetuate female out-migration by sanctioning a daughter's leaving home for her own reasons.

Whatever the combination of forces at work, by the 1910s and 1920s going to the Boston States had taken on a life of its own. Boston itself, replete with all the wonders of the twentieth century, from subways to motion picture palaces to skyscrapers, was a powerful attraction to Maritimers, some of whom still lived in homes without electricity or indoor plumbing. Some historians, struck by the repeated comments of older residents that "everyone went to Boston" in those years, argue that out-migration itself was as much a product of a sense of regional inferiority as a response to changing economic conditions.[8] However, it is important to note that this sense of backwardness was itself the product of the unevenness of capitalist development, the somewhat invidious comparison between a centre of wealth and advancement and a peripheral region that supplied resources, including labour, to build these centres. The perception among Maritime youth in the early twentieth century that Boston was a Mecca for employment, excitement, and independence also implies its converse: that the Maritimes provinces, particularly their rural areas and small towns, were places of limited opportunity, lower wages, and continued dependence on multiple jobs and seasonal work for economic survival. For single women in the 1910s and 1920s, the comparison had an added dimension. The rapid expansion of female employment in cities like Boston offered Maritime daughters an unprecedented opportunity to act in freedom from a patriarchal family structure, at least for the period in their lives between high school and marriage.

There were other modern metropolises like Boston across North America and Europe in the early twentieth century, a situation that suggests the possibility that young women may have followed a similar cityward migration in search of similar independence throughout the Western industrial world. One of the most important benefits of integrating the female experience into a discussion of Maritime out-migration may be the discovery of how this regional phenomenon fits into the larger field of migration studies. Population movements have occurred throughout history, but the specific timing and characteristics of these movements have varied with the contexts in which they took place. A major component of Maritime out-migration between 1860 and 1930 was the rural-to-urban movement of single women, first as part of a strategy of family response to the need for cash money and, over time, more as an effort among daughters to exercise some autonomy for a period of their lives. How did their behaviour compare to that of young women in other parts of the Western world?

The collaborative work of Louise Tilly and Joan Scott on young women who went to work in the cities of western Europe in the nineteenth and early twentieth centuries offers convincing evidence that the rural-to-urban migration of single women was a far-reaching phenomenon. It also connects this migration to changing economic conditions through the decisions made by rural and working-class families in response to the dislocations of capitalist development. The terms they used – "family wage economy" to describe the earlier period of female urban migration, when daughters earned wages for their families, and "family consumer economy" to depict a later period when daughters exercised more control over their own income – encapsulate the same transformation of the nature of female migration that took place in the Maritime provinces. This comparison in no way negates the unique aspects of Maritime out-migration: the seasonal nature of work in the traditional Maritime economy of staples production; the role of Confederation in fixing the locus of political and economic power outside the region; the well-established cultural and commercial connections with New England, which encouraged a cross-border migration pattern. What it does reveal is the critical importance of a daughter's paid labour to rural families, whether in eastern Canada or western Europe, as these families adapted their economic behaviour to the challenges of industrialization. It also reveals that wherever daughters worked for wages, they began to demand and exercise independence from familial control. Alice, Clara, and Jennie Peck and all their female compatriots were not only actors in Maritimes history; they were part of a process taking place all over Europe and North America in the late nineteenth and early twentieth centuries.

APPENDIX A

Domestic and Agricultural Production in the Maritimes, 1871–1891

Table A.1
Domestic cloth production in the Maritime provinces, 1871–91 (in yards)

	1871	1881	1891
New Brunswick	1,125,069	859,928	451,543
Nova Scotia	1,587,990	1,397,855	760,218
Prince Edward Island*		544,770	411,095

Source: Census of Canada, 1870–71 (Ottawa: I.B. Taylor, 1873); Census of Canada, 1880–81 (Ottawa: Maclean, Roger, 1882–85); Census of Canada, 1890–91 (Ottawa: S.E. Dawson, 1893–97).
Note:
* Prince Edward Island was not included in the 1871 census.

Table A.2
Grain production* in the Maritime provinces, 1871–91 (in bushels)

	1871	1881	1891
New Brunswick	4,602,133	5,527,323	4,499,925
Nova Scotia	3,005,139	3,031,929	2,117,989
Prince Edward Island**		4,297,941	3,771,128

Source: Census of Canada, 1870–71; Census of Canada, 1880–81; Census of Canada, 1890–91.
Notes:
* Grain includes spring wheat, fall wheat, barley, oats, rye, buckwheat, and corn.
** Prince Edward Island was not included in the 1871 census.

Table A.3
Production of apples in the Maritime provinces, 1871–91 (in bushels)

	1871	1881	1891
New Brunswick	126,395	231,096	259,615
Nova Scotia	342,531	908,519	1,051,592
Prince Edward Island*		31,501	52,081

Source: Census of Canada, 1870–71; Census of Canada, 1880–81; Census of Canada, 1890–91.
Note:
* Prince Edward Island was not included in the 1871 census.

Table A.4
Production of butter in the Maritime provinces, 1871–91 (in pounds)

	1871	1881	1891
New Brunswick	126,395	231,096	259,615
Nova Scotia	342,531	908,519	1,051,592
Prince Edward Island*		31,501	52,018

Source: Census of Canada, 1870–71; Census of Canada, 1880–81; Census of Canada, 1890–91.
Note:
* Prince Edward Island was not included in the 1871 census.

APPENDIX B

Occupation Tables

Table B.1

Occupations of single Maritime-born women living in Boston, 1880

Occupational group/Occupation	Number	(%)
PROFESSIONAL		
Actress	1	
Artist	5	
Keeper of insane asylum	1	
Lab worker	1	
Lawyer	1	
Librarian	2	
Music teacher	8	
Teacher	9	
Trained nurse	55	
Subtotal	83	(2.2)
CLERICAL		
Bookkeeper	5	
Cashier	4	
Clerk	3	
Copyist	2	
Dentist office helper	1	
Runs employment office	1	
Stenographer	1	
Telegraph operator	3	
Subtotal	20	(.5)
OWNER/MANAGER–BUSINESS		
Fancy goods merchant	1	
Hat merchant	1	
Liquor merchant	1	

Table B.1 *(continued)*

Occupational group/Occupation	Number	(%)
Tobacconist	1	
Subtotal	4	(.1)
SALES		
Saleswoman – bakery	3	
Saleswoman – candy	1	
Saleswoman – clothing	2	
Saleswoman – dry goods	5	
Saleswoman – fancy goods	1	
Saleswoman – hardware	2	
Saleswoman – medicines	1	
Saleswoman – sewing machines	1	
Saleswoman – shoes	1	
Saleswoman – tobacco	2	
Saleswoman – unspecified	32	
Saleswoman – variety	1	
Subtotal	52	(1.4)
DOMESTIC SERVICE		
Companion	1	
Cook	12	
Domestic servant	2,333	
Governess	1	
Housekeeper	37	
Nurse – family	11	
Nurse girl	6	
Servant – not live-in	27	
Subtotal	2,428	(65.4)
SERVICE – INSTITUTION		
Boarding-house keeper	19	
Cook – boarding-house	11	
Cook – hotel	7	
Cook – restaurant	8	
Houseworker – restaurant	1	
Laundress – hotel	5	
Seamstress – hotel	1	
Servant – hotel	34	
Servant – institution	37	
Waitress – hotel	5	
Waitress – restaurant	18	
Waitress – saloon	11	
Subtotal	379	(10.2)
SERVICE – OTHER		
Hairdresser	2	
Janitress	1	
Laundress	14	
Subtotal	17	(.5)
SEWING TRADES		
Coat maker	28	
Dressmaker	299	
Lace maker	2	

Table B.1 (continued)

Occupational group/Occupation	Number	(%)
Milliner	19	
Pants maker	6	
Seamstress	99	
Sewing machine operator	9	
Shirt maker	4	
Suspenders maker	1	
Tailoress	173	
Underwear maker	2	
Vest maker	24	
Subtotal	666	(17.9)
OTHER MANUFACTURES		
Baker	5	
Bookbinder	3	
Carper maker	9	
Cigar maker	4	
Confectioner	3	
Feather renovator	1	
Food canner	1	
Musical instrument maker	1	
Nail maker	1	
Potter	1	
Rope braid maker	3	
Rubber factory worker	5	
Silk mill worker	4	
Straw worker	3	
Upholsterer	2	
Subtotal	46	(1.2)
SHOE MANUFACTURING		
Shoe buttonholder	1	
Shoe stitcher	2	
Shoe vamper	1	
Shoe worker – general	3	
Subtotal	7	(.2)
PRINTING TRADES		
Compositor	4	
Lithographer	1	
Map maker	1	
Photographer	3	
Printer	2	
Subtotal	11	(.3)
TOTAL	3,713	(99.9)*

Source: US Census of Population, 1880, Schedule no. 1: Boston, Suffolk County,
Massachusetts, in National Archives and Records Service, Tenth Census of the United
States, 1880 (Washington: NARS, 1960), reels 552–62.
Note:
* Does not add up to 100.0 because percentage figures are rounded off.

Table B.2
Occupations of single English-Canadian women living in Boston, 1910

Occupational group/Occupation	Number	(%)
RELIGIOUS WORK		
Missionary	66	
Nun	16	
Subtotal	82	(1.3)
PROFESSIONAL		
Actress	3	
Artist	7	
Author	1	
Designer	2	
Journalist	4	
Librarian	3	
Music teacher	16	
Musician	1	
Physician	3	
Social Worker	8	
Teacher	37	
Trained/student nurse	767	
Translator	3	
Subtotal	855	(13.1)
CLERICAL WORK		
Bookkeeper	163	
Cashier	55	
Clerical worker	60	
Correspondent	1	
Government clerk	19	
Office secretary	16	
Stenographer	150	
Telegraph operator	13	
Telephone operator	37	
Typewriter	8	
Subtotal	522	(8.0)
OWNER/MANAGER – BUSINESS		
Boarding-house/lodging-house keeper	167	
Brokerage manager	1	
China merchant	1	
Drug merchant	2	
Dry goods merchant	11	
Fur merchant	1	
Grocer	7	
Hardware merchant	1	
Newspaper merchant	2	
Photo studio manager	1	
Runs dress shop	4	
Runs variety store	1	
Subtotal	206	(3.2)
SALES		
Buyer – department store	9	

Table B.2 (continued)

Occupational group/Occupation	Number	(%)
Saleswoman – bakery	29	
Saleswoman – books/stationery	11	
Saleswoman – boots/shoes	4	
Saleswoman – candy	13	
Saleswoman – clothing	9	
Saleswoman – dept. store	69	
Saleswoman – drugs/tobacco	4	
Saleswoman – dry goods	69	
Saleswoman – fancy goods	1	
Saleswoman – furniture	1	
Saleswoman – furs	1	
Saleswoman – groceries	13	
Saleswoman – hardware	1	
Saleswoman – hats	7	
Saleswoman – junk	1	
Saleswoman – newspapers	5	
Saleswoman – unspecified	24	
Subtotal	273	(4.2)
DOMESTIC SERVICE		
Companion	4	
Cook – family	158	
Domestic servant	1,706	
Governess	3	
Housekeeper	108	
Nurse – family	77	
Nurse girl	48	
Servant – not live-in	182	
Subtotal	2,286	(35.1)
SERVICE – INSTITUTIONAL		
Cook – boarding-house	9	
Cook – hotel/institution	17	
Cook – restaurant	35	
House worker – restaurant	3	
Kitchen girl – hotel	3	
Laundress – boarding-house	1	
Laundress – hotel	24	
Meat cook – hotel	9	
Meat cook – restaurant	1	
Pastry cook – hotel	2	
Pastry cook – restaurant	1	
Seamstress – hotel	4	
Servant – boarding-house/lodging-house	96	
Servant – hotel	66	
Servant – institution	77	
Waitress – hotel	73	
Waitress – restaurant	346	
Waitress – saloon	2	
Subtotal	769	(11.8)

Table B.2 *(continued)*

Occupational group/Occupation	Number	(%)
SERVICE – OTHER		
Bathhouse employee	5	
Dentist office helper	2	
Hairdresser	20	
Janitress	9	
Laboratory worker	1	
Laundress	84	
Manicurist	18	
Matron – railroad station	2	
Wig maker	1	
Subtotal	142	(2.2)
OTHER NON-MANUFACTURING		
Demonstrator	4	
Employment agent	1	
Floor walker	1	
Loan collector	3	
Model	2	
Show employee	3	
Subtotal	14	(.2)
FOOD PRODUCTION		
Baker	9	
Coffee mill worker	2	
Confectioner	37	
Food canner	2	
Subtotal	50	(.8)
SHOE MANUFACTURING		
Button lace maker	1	
Shoe cememter	1	
Shoe forewomen	3	
Shoe labeller	4	
Shoe liner	1	
Shoe packer	2	
Shoe stayer	1	
Shoe stitcher	27	
Shoe vamper	1	
Shoe worker – general	18	
Top stitcher	3	
Subtotal	62	(1.0)
SEWING TRADES		
Cloth cutter	1	
Coat maker	3	
Dressmaker	585	
Lace maker	6	
Milliner	90	
Pants maker	4	
Seamstress	186	
Sewing machine operator	50	
Shirt maker	10	

Table B.2 *(continued)*

Occupational group/Occupation	Number	(%)
Suspenders maker	16	
Tailoress	89	
Umbrella maker	2	
Underwear maker	8	
Vest maker	5	
Subtotal	1,055	(16.2)
TEXTILE MANUFACTURING		
Cotton mill worker	3	
Cotton presser	1	
Dye house worker	1	
Knitting mill worker	6	
Rope braid worker	1	
Wool weaver	2	
Woollen mill worker	1	
Subtotal	15	(.2)
PRINTING TRADES		
Compositor	25	
Engraver	1	
Photo finisher	1	
Photographer	1	
Printer	6	
Proofreader	8	
Retoucher	2	
Stereotyper	1	
Subtotal	45	(.7)
OTHER MANUFACTURING		
Bookbinder	16	
Box maker	23	
Broom brush maker	4	
Card maker	1	
Carpet maker	4	
Chair caner	1	
Cigar maker	1	
Electrical winder	2	
Electrical worker	10	
Factory inspector	1	
Feather renovator	1	
Forewoman – electrical work	1	
Forewoman – unspecified	10	
Frame maker	1	
Fur worker	3	
Glass worker	1	
Inspector – electrical work	1	
Iron/steel worker	2	
Jeweller	1	
Lamp maker	8	
Lamp tester	1	
Mattress maker	2	

Table B.2 *(continued)*

Occupational group/Occupation	Number	(%)
Musical instrument maker	2	
Paper mill worker	1	
Potter	2	
Purse maker	2	
Razor factory worker	15	
Rubber factory worker	10	
Tobacco factory worker	1	
Upholsterer	3	
Window shade maker	10	
Wire coverer	1	
Subtotal	142	(2.2)
TOTAL	6,518	(100.2)*

Source: US Census of Population, 1910, Schedule no. 1: Boston, Suffolk County, Massachusetts, in US National Archives and Records Service, *Thirteenth Census of the United States, 1910* (Washington: NARS, 1982), reels 614–26.

Note:

* Does not add up to 100.0 because percentage figures are rounded off.

Table B.3
Occupations of single English-Canadian women living in Boston, 1920

Occupational group/Occupation	Number	(%)
RELIGIOUS WORK		
Clergywoman	1	
Missionary	11	
Nun	100	
Subtotal	112	(2.4)
PROFESSIONAL		
Accountant	6	
Actress	1	
Artist	7	
Dance teacher	4	
Dentist	1	
Designer	7	
Engineer	1	
Journalist	6	
Librarian	1	
Keeper of the insane	19	
Matron – unspecified	3	
Music teacher	10	
Musician	1	
Physician	3	
School administrator	2	
Social worker	17	
Teacher	41	
Trained/student nurse	731	
Subtotal	861	(18.7)
CLERICAL		
Bookkeeper	113	
Cashier	47	
Clerical worker	112	
Copyist	3	
Government clerk	1	
Office secretary	34	
Stenographer	141	
Telegraph operator	8	
Telephone operator	41	
Typist	6	
Subtotal	506	(11.0)
OWNER/MANAGER – BUSINESS		
Antique dealer	2	
Boarding-house/lodging-house keeper	115	
China merchant	1	
Dry goods merchant	6	
Fancy goods merchant	1	
Fur merchant	1	
Grocer	3	
Real estate merchant	3	
Runs bakery	2	

Table B.3 *(continued)*

Occupational group/Occupation	Number	(%)
Runs restaurant	10	
Storekeeper – unspecified	9	
Subtotal	153	(3.3)
SALES		
Advertising agent	1	
Buyer – dept. store	7	
Commercial traveller	1	
Saleswoman – art	2	
Saleswoman – bakery	7	
Saleswoman – books/stationery	2	
Saleswoman – candy	4	
Saleswoman – china	1	
Saleswoman – clothing	9	
Saleswoman – corsets	1	
Saleswoman – dept. store	93	
Saleswoman – drugs/tobacco	6	
Saleswoman – dry goods	29	
Saleswoman – fancy goods	1	
Saleswoman – furniture	1	
Saleswoman – furs	4	
Saleswoman – groceries	19	
Saleswoman – hair	1	
Saleswoman – hardware	1	
Saleswoman – hats	1	
Saleswoman – jewellery	3	
Saleswoman – musical instruments	4	
Saleswoman – newspapers	2	
Saleswoman – novelties	2	
Saleswoman – unspecified	28	
Subtotal	230	(5.0)
DOMESTIC SERVICE		
Companion	14	
Cook – family	115	
Domestic servant*	810	
Governess	5	
Housekeeper	89	
Nurse – family	75	
Servant – not live-in	135	
Subtotal	1,243	(27.1)
SERVICE – INSTITUTIONAL		
Cook – boarding-house	2	
Cook – hotel/other institution	18	
Cook – restaurant	21	
Dish washer – hotel	2	
Hat check girl	14	
House worker – restaurant	7	
Kitchen girl – hotel	1	

Table B.3 *(continued)*

Occupational group/Occupation	Number	(%)
Laundress – boarding-house	1	
Laundress – hotel	14	
Pastry cook – restaurant	2	
Seamstress – hotel	3	
Servant – boarding-house	23	
Servant – hotel	51	
Servant – institution	73	
Stewardess	2	
Waitress – hotel	56	
Waitress – restaurant	214	
Subtotal	504	(11.0)
SERVICE – OTHER		
Bathhouse employee	9	
Charity worker	8	
Dentist office helper	1	
Employment agency worker	2	
Hairdresser	19	
Janitress	10	
Laundress	53	
Manicurist	10	
Matron – railroad station	5	
Usher – movie theatre	1	
Subtotal	118	(2.6)
OTHER NON-MANUFACTURING		
Demonstrator	2	
Floor walker	1	
Laboratory worker	2	
Loan collector	1	
Messenger	4	
Model	2	
Show employee	1	
Subtotal	13	(0.3)
SHOE MANUFACTURING		
Forewoman – shoe factory	1	
Heel worker	1	
Shoe binder	1	
Shoe caser	1	
Shoe cleaner	1	
Shoe cutter	2	
Shoe finisher	2	
Shoe laster	2	
Shoe packer	4	
Shoe paster	1	
Shoe stitcher	52	
Shoe trimmer	1	
Shoe turner	2	
Shoe worker – general	20	

Table B.3 *(continued)*

Occupational group/Occupation	Number	(%)
Shoe vamper	1	
Skiver	1	
Subtotal	93	(2.0)
SEWING TRADES		
Coat maker	3	
Dressmaker	263	
Glove maker	1	
Hoopskirt maker	3	
Milliner	38	
Seamstress	77	
Sewing machine operator	28	
Shipper – cloth factory	1	
Shirt maker	9	
Suspender maker	7	
Tailoress	38	
Underwear maker	5	
Vest maker	1	
Subtotal	474	(10.3)
TEXTILE MANUFACTURING		
Cotton mill worker	2	
Cotton weaver	2	
Dye house worker	1	
Knitting mill worker	4	
Silk mill worker	6	
Thread maker	1	
Woollen mill worker	2	
Subtotal	18	(0.4)
PRINTING		
Compositor	6	
Lithographer	1	
Printer	6	
Proof reader	1	
Retoucher	2	
Subtotal	16	(0.3)
OTHER MANUFACTURING		
Artificial flower maker	1	
Baker	3	
Bookbinder	11	
Box maker	21	
Broom/brush maker	6	
Button maker	3	
Card maker	1	
Chemical factory worker	2	
Coffee mill worker	4	
Confectioner	33	
Drug/patent medicine bottler	4	
Electrical winder	6	
Electrical worker	17	

Table B.3 *(continued)*

Occupational group/Occupation	Number	(%)
Factory inspector	13	
Factory worker – unspecified	33	
Forewoman – unspecified	19	
Frame maker	1	
Fur worker	3	
Glass worker	1	
Iron/steel worker	1	
Jeweller	1	
Machinist	2	
Mattress maker	3	
Medical equipment worker	1	
Metal polisher	1	
Paper mill worker	2	
Potter	1	
Purse maker	3	
Razor factory worker	23	
Rubber factory worker	22	
Sausage maker	1	
Straw worker	1	
Tire maker/inspector	1	
Upholsterer	1	
Watchmaker/repairer	1	
Window shade maker	7	
Subtotal	254	(5.5)
TOTAL	4,595	(99.5)**

Source: us Census of Population, 1920, Schedule no. 1: Boston, Suffolk County, Massachusetts, in us National Archives and Records Service, *Thirteenth Census of the United States, 1920* (Washington: NARS, 1992), reels 728–43.

Notes:

* The following job descriptions were grouped together under the title "domestic servant": maid, parlour maid, chambermaid, waitress (private home), laundress (private home).

** Does not add up to 100 per cent because percentage figures are rounded off.

Notes

INTRODUCTION

1 *Herald* (Halifax), 31 December 1904.
2 *Daily News* (Amherst, NS), 3 October 1898.
3 "Prince Edward Isle Adieu," in Gary Burrill, *Away: Maritimers in Massachusetts, Ontario, and Alberta: An Oral History of Leaving Home* (Montreal: McGill-Queen's University Press, 1992), 1.
4 Patricia Thornton, "The Problem of Out-migration from Atlantic Canada, 1871–1921: A New Look," *Acadiensis* 15, no. 1 (autumn 1985): 18.
5 Alan Alexander Brookes, "The Exodus: Migration from the Maritime Provinces to Boston during the Second Half of the Nineteenth Century" (PhD diss., University of New Brunswick, 1978), 9.
6 Kari Levitt, *Population Movements in the Atlantic Provinces* (Fredericton: Atlantic Provinces Economic Growth Council, 1960), 3.
7 Thornton, "The Problem of Out-migration," 3.
8 The subject of economic decline and the failure of indigenous industrial development is an oft-addressed topic among historians of the Maritime region. They disagree among themselves about both the cause and timing of that decline but seem to share the opinion that by 1930 the Maritimes lagged far behind central Canada in industrial output and had surrendered much of their industrial base to external ownership. A good general discussion of the subject, with statistics to demonstrate the region's economic decline, is David Alexander's "Economic Growth in the Atlantic Region, 1880 to 1940," *Acadiensis* 8, no. 1

(autumn 1978): 47–76. For a range of interpretations of the causes of regional decline, note the following articles and their respective positions on the debate: Stanley A. Saunders, *Economic History of the Maritime Provinces* (Fredericton: Acadiensis Press, 1984), an interpretation stressing misuse of staples and the region's "hinterland" relationship to central Canada; Henry Veltmeyer, "The Capitalist Underdevelopment of Atlantic Canada," in *Underdevelopment and Social Movements in Atlantic Canada*, ed. Robert J. Brym and R. James Sacouman (Toronto: New Hogtown Press, 1979), 17–35, a Marxist analysis blaming the failure of the region's economic growth on capitalism's tendency to create uneven regional development; T. William Acheson, "The National Policy and the Industrialization of the Maritimes," *Acadiensis* 1, no. 2 (spring 1972): 3–28, a study that attributes decline to the failure of the region's entrepreneurs; Patricia Thornton, "The Problem of Out-migration," an article suggesting that out-migration from the Maritimes of the young and talented contributed to economic decline.

9 Marcus Lee Hansen and John Bartlett Brebner, *The Mingling of the Canadian and American Peoples* (New Haven: Yale University Press, 1940), 163–4.

10 Brookes, "The Exodus." See, in particular, his chapter on out-migration from Canning, Nova Scotia, one of many communities dependent on the traditional Maritime "wood, wind, and sail" economy. The expression "wood, wind, and sail," used to describe the Maritime staples and carrying trade of the mid-nineteenth century, was coined by D.A. Muise and first appeared in his PhD dissertation, "Elections and Constituencies: Federal Politics in Nova Scotia, 1867–1878" (University of Western Ontario, 1971). He also coined a companion phrase – the age of "iron, steam and rail" – describing the post-Confederation Canadian economy into which the Maritimes were integrated. These succinct descriptions have become an integral part of the lexicon for historians of the region.

11 Veltmeyer, "Capitalist Underdevelopment."

12 Burrill, *Away,* 6–8.

13 Thornton, "The Problem of Outmigration," 3–34.

14 Thornton based her interpretation, in part, on the migration theories of Everett Lee, who first defined the difference between "push" and "pull" factors in decisions to migrate. Lee noted that the less skilled and educated would migrate only when "pushed" away from home by serious negative factors such as crop failures or natural disasters while the better-trained would also respond to the "pull" of better wages or job opportunities in another region. See Everett Lee, "A Theory of Migration," *Demography* 3 (1966): 47, 56.

15 Thornton, "The Problem of Out-migration," 18–19.

16 Hansen and Brebner, *Mingling*, 163.

17 Thornton, "The Problem of Out-migration," 18–19.

18 Brookes noted that in Boston in 1880 there were 1,682 single men and 1,533 single women living as boarders as well as 2,568 persons living with families as domestic servants. Since all but a tiny minority of servants were female, it is likely that there were more than 4,000 single women and under 2,000 single men living in the city in 1880. See Brookes, "The Exodus," 176.

19 Thornton, "The Problem of Out-migration," 20.

20 Brookes, "The Exodus," 127.

21 Hansen and Brebner, *Mingling*, 163–4.

22 Thornton, "The Problem of Out-migration," 20.

23 Brookes, "The Exodus," 127.

24 Fiona K. Bellerive, "Light upon the Shadows of Exodus: Maritime Women and the Boston YWCA" (Masters thesis, Dalhousie University, 1994).

25 Ibid., vi.

26 See, for example: T.W. Acheson, "New Brunswick Agriculture at the End of the Colonial Era: A Reassessment," *Acadiensis* 22, no. 2 (spring 1993): 5–26; Rusty Bittermann, "The Hierarchy of the Soil: Land and Labour in a 19th Century Cape Breton Community," *Acadiensis* 18, no. 1 (autumn 1988): 33–55; Rusty Bittermann, Robert MacKinnon, and Graeme Wynn, "Of Inequality and Interdependence in the Nova Scotian Countryside, 1850–70," *Canadian Historical Review*, 74. no. 1 (March 1993): 1–43; Danny Samson, "Dependency and Rural Industry: Inverness, Nova Scotia, 1899–1915," in *Contested Countryside: Rural Workers and Modern Society in Atlantic Canada, 1800–1950*, ed. Danny Samson (Fredericton, Acadiensis Press, 1994), 105–49; and Steven Maynard, "Between Farm and Factory: The Productive Household and Capitalist Transformation of the Maritime Countryside, Hopewell, Nova Scotia, 1869–1890," in ibid., 70–104.

27 Of the three Maritime provinces, New Brunswick had the smallest percentage of its land under cultivation, and throughout much of the nineteenth century the extraction of forest products was the most valuable economic activity of the province. Nevertheless, according to Graeme Wynn, "in 1851, farmers accounted for more than half of those whose occupations were listed by the New Brunswick census." Graeme Wynn, *Timber Colony: A Historical Geography of Early Nineteenth-Century New Brunswick* (Toronto: University of Toronto Press, 1981), 8. Meanwhile, Andrew Hill Clark wrote about Prince Edward Island: "In the middle of the nineteenth century the population of the island was overwhelming

rural...the rural total [of the population] must have substantially exceeded 90 per cent." Andrew Hill Clark, *Three Centuries and the Island: A Historical Geography of Settlement and Agriculture in Prince Edward Island, Canada* (Toronto: University of Toronto Press, 1959), 128.

28 Bittermann, MacKinnon, Wynn, "Of Inequality and Interdependence," 23–5.

29 In a 1922 history of Inverness County, Nova Scotia, John L. MacDougall wrote, "Farmers, as a rule, have to avail themselves of various other means of adding to their income. Some near the shore combine farming and fishing. Some are farmers and carpenters. Some find work at industrial centres. Some sell railway ties, pit props, timber and firewood. And then by earning a little here and a little there, and by the constant practice of careful economy, they are able to enjoy the necessaries of life, but by no means many of its luxuries." John L. MacDougall, *History of Inverness County*, quoted in Samson, "Dependency and Rural Industry," 1.

30 Bittermann, MacKinnon, Wynn, "Of Inequality and Interdependence," passim.

31 Scholars first observed the workings of the family economy in the peasant families of Europe from the sixteenth through the nineteenth centuries, as capitalism transformed social and economic relations in the European countryside and survival on farms was increasingly difficult for all but those with land holdings large enough to produce a surplus for commercial sale. In recent years, American social historians have demonstrated that both rural and urban poor families, faced with the commercialization of agriculture and industrial capitalist development in nineteenth-century North America, used similar strategies to survive sub-living wages and inadequate farm production. For a representative collection on the peasant family or household as an economic unit see Richard Wall, Jean Robin, and Peter Laslett, eds., *Family Forms in Historical Europe* (Cambridge: Cambridge University Press, 1983). For a synthesis of the findings of historians on how families in Europe and North America adapted the family economy to an urban, industrial setting, see Michael Anderson, *Approaches to the History of the Western Family, 1500–1914* (London: Macmillan, 1984), 78–80. Some examples of how Canadian rural and urban families used the family economy as a survival strategy are John Bullen, "Hidden Workers: Child Labour and the Family Economy in Late Nineteenth-Century Urban Ontario," *Labour/Le Travail* 18 (fall 1986): 163–87; Bettina Bradbury, "The Family Economy and Work in an Industrializing City: Montreal in the 1870s," *Canadian Historical Association Historical Papers* (1979): 71–96; Chad Gaffield, "Wage Labour, Industrialization, and the Origins of the Modern Family," in *The Family: Changing Trends in Canada*, ed. Maureen Baker (Toronto: McGraw-Hill Ryerson, 1984), 23–40; and Marjorie

Griffin Cohen, *Women's Work, Markets, and Economic Development in Nineteenth-Century Ontario* (Toronto: University of Toronto Press, 1988).

32 See Louisa Collins's diary excerpted in Margaret Conrad, Toni Laidlaw, and Donna Smyth, *No Place Like Home: Diaries and Letters of Nova Scotia Women, 1771–1938* (Halifax: Formac, 1988), 68.

33 "With Katie Margaret Gillis, Mabou Coal Mines," *Cape Breton's Magazine* no. 38: 11.

34 There are numerous references to the specific tasks expected of rural women in the Maritimes and to their options for paid work. See, for example, Stephen Maynard, "On the Market's Edge: The Productive Household and the Capitalist Transformation of the Maritime Countryside, Hopewell, Nova Scotia, 1870–1890," unpublished paper, 1990, 7–8. Bittermann, "Of Inequality and Interdependence," 30; and the diaries of Louisa Collins and Rebecca Chase Kinsman Ells excerpted in Conrad, Laidlaw, and Smyth, *No Place Like Home*, 65–78, 207–25.

35 Thornton, "The Problem of Out-migration," 20.

36 US Census Office, *Tenth Census (1880)*, 3 vols (Washington: Government Printing Office, 1883), 1:492. The top five Massachusetts cities attracting female Maritimers in 1885, according to the Massachusetts state census, were: Boston, Cambridge, Lynn, Gloucester, and Chelsea. See Carroll D. Wright, *The Census of Massachusetts, 1885*, 3 vols (Boston: Wright and Potter, 1887–88), vol. 1, pt. 1, 490–563.

37 Betsy Beattie, "Dutiful Daughters: Maritime-Born Women in New England in the Late Nineteenth Century," *Retrospection* 2 (1989): 22.

38 Betsy Beattie, "'Going Up to Lynn:' Single Maritime-Born Women in Lynn, Massachusetts, 1879–1930," *Acadiensis* 23, no. 1 (Autumn 1992): 68.

39 Albert Kennedy, "'The Provincials,' with an Introduction by Alan A. Brookes," *Acadiensis* 4, no. 2 (spring 1975): 89, 91, 94.

40 Francesco Codasco, *The Immigrant Woman in North America: An Annotated Bibliography of Selected References* (Metuchen, NJ: Scarecrow Press, 1985); Suzanne Sinké, "A Historiography of Immigrant Women in the Nineteenth and Early Twentieth Centuries," *Ethnic Forum* 9, nos 1–2 (1989): 122–45; Sydney Stahl Weinberg, "The Treatment of Women in Immigration History: A Call for Change," *Journal of American Ethnic History* 11, no. 4 (summer 1992): 25–46; Maxine Schwartz Seller, *Immigrant Women*, 2nd ed. (Albany: State University of New York Press, 1994), 345–69.

41 Seller, *Immigrant Women*, 3.

42 Ibid.

43 Studies of single women immigrants in domestic service include: Joy K. Lintelman, "'America Is the Woman's Promised Land': Swedish Immigrant Women and American Domestic Service," *Journal of American Ethnic History* 8, no. 2 (spring 1989): 9–23; Carl Ross and K. Marianne

Wargelin-Brown, eds, *Women Who Dared: The History of Finnish American Women* (St Paul, MN: Immigration History Research Center, 1986); Varpu Lindström-Best, "'I Won't Be a Slave': Finnish Domestics in Canada," in *Looking into My Sister's Eyes: An Exploration in Women's History*, ed. Jean Burnet (Toronto: Multicultural History Society of Ontario, 1986), 44–50; Suzanne Sinké, "'Send News Soon': Letters from German Immigrant Women" (paper presented at the Missouri Valley History Conference, Omaha, NB, March 1988); Carole Groneman, "Immigrant Women in Mid-Nineteenth-Century New York: The Irish Women's Experience," *Journal of Urban History* 4, no. 3 (1978): 255–73; and Marilyn Barber, "Sunny Ontario for British Girls," in *Looking into My Sister's Eyes*, ed. Burnet, 55–71. One exception to the pattern of single women migrants as domestic servants was the group of British hosiery knitters who were recruited by Penman's Company to work in their mill in Paris, Ontario, in the early twentieth century. See Joy Parr, *The Gender of Breadwinners: Women, Men, and Change in Two Industrial Towns, 1880–1950* (Toronto: University of Toronto Press, 1990).

44 David Katzman, *Seven Days a Week: Women and Domestic Service in Industrializing America* (New York: Oxford University Press, 1978), 44.

45 Sinké, "A Historiography of Immigrant Women," 125.

46 Groneman, "Working-Class Immigrant Women," 257.

47 Janet A. Nolan, *Ourselves Alone: Women's Emigration from Ireland, 1885–1920* (Lexington: University of Kentucky Press, 1989), 77–8.

48 In the second half of the nineteenth century, according to Alice Kessler-Harris, for working-class families, "high unemployment rates, seasonal work, technological dislocation, and real wages that barely kept pace with rising living costs all encouraged women to seek jobs." In a Canadian context, Bettina Bradbury documented the common practice of sons and daughters working for wages among the working class of Montreal in the 1870s. See Alice Kessler-Harris, *Out to Work: A History of Wage-Earning Women in the United States* (New York: Oxford University Press, 1982), 122; Bradbury, "Family Economy," 77–86.

49 Bettina Bradbury, "Women and Wage Labour in a Period of Transition: Montreal, 1861–1881," *Histoire sociale/Social History* 17, no. 33 (May 1984): 115.

50 Leslie Tentler, *Wage-Earning Women, Industrial Work, and Family Life in the United States, 1900–1930* (New York: Oxford University Press, 1979), 89.

51 E.G. Ravenstein, quoted in Lee, "A Theory of Migration," 47–8.

52 See, for example, Adna Ferrin Weber, *The Growth of Cities in the Nineteenth Century: A Study in Statistics* (New York: Macmillan, 1899), 276–80, and Donald J. Bogue, *Principles of Demography* (New York: John Wiley, 1969), 169. A third study, published in 1938, presented somewhat more ambiguous conclusions. Dorothy Thomas, in *Research*

Memorandum on Migration Differentials (New York: Social Science Research Council, 1938), summarized the findings of studies on gender differences in short-distance, rural-to-urban migrations. She concluded: "The available data suggest that the 'rural exodus' had been sex-selective of females, particularly in the young adult ages, but that 'urbanization' *per se* is not selective of females" (68).

53 Abel Chatelain, "Migrations et domesticité feminine urbaine en France, XVIII–XXe siècles," *Revue d'histoire économique et sociale* 47, no. 4 (1969): 502–28.

54 Theresa M. McBride, "The Long Road Home: Women's Work and Industrialization," in *Becoming Visible: Women in European History*, ed. Renate Bridenthal and Claudia Koonz (Boston: Houghton Mifflin, 1977), 287.

55 Ibid., 287–8.

56 See Kessler-Harris, *Out to Work*; Elyce J. Rotella, *From Home to Office: U.S. Women's Work, 1870–1930* (Ann Arbor, MI: UMI Research Press, 1981); Veronica Strong-Boag, *The New Day Recalled: Lives of Girls and Women in English Canada, 1919–1939* (Toronto: Copp Clark Pitman, 1988).

57 Anderson, *Approaches to the History of the Western Family*, 93.

58 Joan W. Scott and Louise A. Tilly, "Women's Work and the Family in Nineteenth-Century Europe," *Comparative Studies in Society and History* 17 (1975): 36–64.

59 The traditional Marxist interpretation, for example, stressed that the change in mode and location of production deprived women of a role in family production, thus reducing their power and lowering their position in the family. Scott and Tilly quote Friedrich Engels as claiming that industrial capitalism excluded women from "participation in social production," thereby reducing their status to that of a servant. Scott and Tilly argued that the family, and particularly women in the family, were far more adaptive than Engels suggested. Those women no longer employed in home production or needed for home maintenance went out to find wage work as a means of contributing to the family economy. See Scott and Tilly, "Women's Work," 42.

60 Ibid., 52–3.

61 William Josiah Goode, *World Revolution and Family Patterns* (New York: Free Press, 1963), 56.

62 Scott and Tilly, "Women's Work," 42.

63 Ibid.

64 Louise A. Tilly and Joan W. Scott, *Women, Work, and Family* (New York: Holt, Rinehart and Winston, 1978).

65 See, for example, reviews by Neil J. Smelser, in *Journal of Economic History* 39, no. 2 (1979): 501–2, and Noelle Whiteside, in *Sociological Review* 29, no. 1 (1981): 394–6.

66 Heidi I. Hartmann, "The Family as the Locus of Gender, Class, and Political Struggle: The Example of Housework," *Signs: Journal of Women in Culture and Society* 6, no. 3 (Spring 1981): 368.

67 Cohen, *Women's Work*, 29–92.

68 Joanne J. Meyerowitz, *Women Adrift: Independent Wage Earners in Chicago, 1880–1930* (Chicago: University of Chicago Press, 1988), 1–2.

69 Ibid., 5.

70 In *Women Adrift*, Meyerowitz argued that women migrants, far from feeling connected to a family back home, were "bereft of family support and confronted with poverty." To counter this isolation they created informal networks or "subcultures" of wage-earning women and working-class women, "not simply as support and survival networks but also as potential arenas for change, areas where women sometimes forged new standards of behavior that defied the standards of employers, family, and community leaders." See *Women Adrift*, xxii. In adopting this model of single women's network formation, she echoed the research of historians such as Susan Porter Benson, in *Counter Cultures: Saleswomen, Managers, and Customers in American Department Stores, 1890–1940* (Urbana: University of Illinois Press, 1986), and Barbara Melosh, in *"Physician's Hand": Work Culture and Conflict in American Nursing* (Philadelphia: Temple University Press, 1982). However, most of these studies of female work cultures focus on the early years of the twentieth century, when there were more employment choices for women, and, if one applies the Tilly – Scott model, the economic structures fit the period of the family consumer economy, when young women were more likely to seek a variety of employment and to be influenced by individual rather than family concerns. Such was not the case in the 1880s, when young women had fewer occupational choices and were more likely to act with family concerns in mind. In short, because she does not address the issue of change over time in the behaviour of women migrants when she introduces the idea of female work cultures, Meyerowitz does not necessarily contradict the ideas presented by Tilly and Scott in *Women, Work, and Family*.

71 A good example of the use of twenty-year generations is the five-generational periodization of nursing history in Kathryn McPherson's, *Bedside Matters: The Transformation of Canadian Nursing, 1900–1990* (Toronto: Oxford University Press, 1996).

CHAPTER ONE

1 Information about the lives of Clara and Alice Peck was taken from an interview with Edgar McKay, Alice Peck McKay's son, in Orono, Maine, 5 May 1986. Information about Joshua Peck and the Peck farm

was taken from the 1871 nominal and agricultural censuses for Nova Scotia.

2 Helen I. Cowan, *British Emigration to British North America: The First Hundred Years*, rev. ed. (Toronto: University of Toronto Press, 1961), 66.

3 There are numerous historical works on geographical mobility in nineteenth-century North America. Among the most important are Peter Knight's study of antebellum Boston, *The Plain People of Boston, 1830–1860: A Study in City Growth* (New York: Oxford University Press, 1971), and David Ward's *Cities and Immigrants: A Geography of Change in Nineteenth-Century America* (New York: Oxford University Press, 1971). Michael Katz addresses the same issue in a Canadian context in his chapter entitled "Transiency and Social Mobility" in *The People of Hamilton, Canada West: Family and Class in a Mid-Nineteenth-Century City* (Cambridge, Mass.: Harvard University Press, 1975), 94–175.

4 Patricia Thornton, "The Problem of Out-migration from Atlantic Canada, 1871–1921: A New Look," *Acadiensis* 15, no. 1 (autumn 1985): 16.

5 *New Brunswick Reporter and Fredericton Advertiser*, 9 April 1869, as cited in Alan Brookes, "Out-migration from the Maritime Provinces, 1860–1900," *Acadiensis* 5, no. 2 (spring 1976): 36.

6 *Morning Chronicle* (Halifax), 22 January 1870.

7 *Acadian Recorder* (Halifax), 24 April 1873, as paraphrased in Alan Brookes, "Out-migration from the Maritime Provinces," 36–7.

8 Thornton, "The Problem of Out-migration," 18.

9 *Record* (Kings County, NB), 12 April 1889.

10 *Daily Examiner* (Charlottetown), 18 March 1880.

11 *Citizen* (Halifax), 8 December 1876.

12 Alan Alexander Brookes, "The Exodus: Migration from the Maritimes to Boston during the Second Half of the Nineteenth Century" (PhD diss., University of New Brunswick, 1978), 9.

13 For a discussion of the end of the proprietor system, see Andrew Hill Clark, *Three Centuries and the Island: A Historical Geography of Settlement and Agriculture in Prince Edward Island, Canada* (Toronto: University of Toronto Press, 1959), 132–3.

14 Graeme Wynn, *Timber Colony: A Historical Geography of Early Nineteenth-Century New Brunswick* (Toronto: University of Toronto Press, 1981), 4.

15 D.A. Muise, "The 1860s: Forging the Bonds of Union," in *The Atlantic Provinces in Confederation*, ed. E.R. Forbes and D.A. Muise (Toronto: University of Toronto Press, 1993), 14.

16 Rusty Bittermann, "Agriculture and Rural Change in Nova Scotia, 1851–1951" (unpublished manuscript), 1.

17 Muise, "The 1860s," 20. For more detailed discussions of the credit relationship between merchant and producer, see Rosemary E. Ohmer, ed.,

Merchant Credit and Labour Strategies in Historical Perspective (Fredericton: Acadiensis Press, 1990).

18 Muise, "The 1860s," 44.

19 Judith Fingard, "The 1880s: Paradoxes of Progress," in *The Atlantic Provinces in Confederation*, ed. Forbes and Muise, 83.

20 Ibid., 83–4.

21 T. William Acheson, "The National Policy and the Industrialization of the Maritimes," *Acadiensis* 1, no. 2 (spring 1972): 3–28.

22 Ibid., 83–4, 97. See also Stanley Saunders's discussion of the economic integration of the Maritime economy with that of the rest of Canada in his *Economic History of the Maritime Region: A Study Prepared for the Royal Commission on Dominion–Provincial Relations* (Ottawa: King's Printer, 1939). Saunders believed that such integration was inevitable, that the centre of Canadian industry was destined by geography to be the valley of the St Lawrence River, and that the integration of regional economies into a single Canadian economy dominated by Quebec and Ontario was in the best interests of the Canadian nation.

23 Brookes, "The Exodus", 83.

24 Ibid., 102.

25 Thornton, "The Problem of Out-migration," 12.

26 Ibid., 18–20.

27 Margaret Conrad, "Chronicles of the Exodus: Myths and Realities for Maritime Canadians in the United States, 1870–1930" (paper presented to the symposium "Four Centuries of Borderland Interaction in the International Region of the Northeast," University of Maine, Orono, November 1987).

28 In the last twenty-five years the field of women's history has burgeoned, and the body of literature on women in nineteenth-century North America is enormous. There is on-going scholarly debate over the role that class, race, and ethnicity played in differentiating the experiences of women, but historians agree that all women's life choices were circumscribed in many ways – socially, economically, politically, legally – because of their gender. Two fine works that explore these themes are Alice Kessler-Harris's history of American women in the paid labour force, *Out to Work: A History of Wage-Earning Women in the United States* (New York: Oxford University Press, 1982); and Alison Prentice, Paula Bourne, Gail Cuthbert Brandt, Beth Light, Wendy Mitchinson, and Naomi Black, *Canadian Women: A History*, 2nd ed. (Toronto: Harcourt Brace, 1996).

29 Rusty Bittermann, Robert A. MacKinnon, and Graeme Wynn, "Of Inequality and Interdependence in the Nova Scotian Countryside, 1850–70," *Canadian Historical Review* 74, no. 1 (March 1993): 4.

30 For a list of research on inequality in rural Maritime communities in the mid-nineteenth century, see note 26 in the Introduction. For a

general discussion of agriculture in the region at mid-century, see Robert MacKinnon and Graeme Wynn, "Nova Scotian Agriculture in the 'Golden Age': A New Look," in *Geographical Perspectives on the Maritime Provinces*, ed. Douglas Day (Halifax: Saint Mary's University, 1988), 47–60.

31 For a discussion of occupational pluralism see L.D. McCann, "'Living a Double Life': Town and Country in the Industrialization of the Maritimes," in ibid., 98. For a more complete description of the family economy as it functioned in the Maritimes at mid-century, see the introduction, ibid., 9–11.

32 In central Canada, for example, Marjorie Griffin Cohen has documented the decline of domestic cloth production by the mid-nineteenth century. In the United States the process evidently began earlier. Alice Kessler-Harris notes a decline in the domestic manufacture of cloth, candles, and brooms by the 1830s. See Marjorie Griffin Cohen, *Women's Work, Markets, and Economic Development in Nineteenth-Century Ontario* (Toronto: University of Toronto Press, 1988), 81, and Kessler-Harris, *Out to Work*, 26–7.

33 In 1871 New Brunswick had six woollen mills and Nova Scotia had eight. By 1891 New Brunswick had seven woollen mills, Nova Scotia had seventeen, and Prince Edward Island had seven. In 1871 New Brunswick was the only Maritime province with cotton mills; it had two. By 1891 New Brunswick had five cotton mills and Nova Scotia had two. See *Census of Canada, 1870–71*, 5 vols (Ottawa: I.B. Taylor, 1873–78), 3:357, 437; *Census of Canada, 1880–81*, 4 vols (Ottawa: Maclean, Roger, 1882–85), 3:391, 485; *Census of Canada, 1890–91*, 4 vols (Ottawa: S.E. Dawson, 1893–97), 3:119–120, 376, 378.

34 Andrew Hill Clark, *Three Centuries and the Island: A Historical Geography of Settlement and Agriculture in Prince Edward Island, Canada* (Toronto: University of Toronto Press, 1959), 186; Robert MacKinnon, "A Century of Farming in Nova Scotia: The Geography of Agriculture, 1851–1951" (paper presented to the Atlantic Canada Workshop, Fredericton, 25 September 1986), 11.

35 M.C. Urquhart and K.A.H. Buckley, *Historical Statistics of Canada* (Cambridge: Cambridge University Press, 1965), 352.

36 Janet Guildford, "'Separate Spheres': The Feminization of Public School Teaching in Nova Scotia, 1838–1880," *Acadiensis* 22, no. 1 (Autumn 1992): 49.

37 Thornton, "The Problem of Outmigration," 19.

38 *Acadian Recorder*, 8 August 1899.

39 *Daily News* (Amherst, NS), 22 August 1899.

40 Provincial Workmen's Association, *Trades Journal*, 23 March 1881; 29 June 1881.

41 *Morning Herald* (Halifax), 13 September 1881.

42 *Morning Chronicle* (Halifax), 5 January 1870.

43 *Nova Scotian* (Halifax), 19 January 1884.

44 *Record* (Kings County, NB), 25 October 1889.

45 *Daily News* (Amherst, NS), 3 October 1898.

46 US Census Office, *Tenth Census (1880)*, 3 vols (Washington: Government Printing Office, 1883), passim.

47 Carroll D. Wright, *The Census of Massachusetts, 1885*, 3 vols (Boston: Wright and Potter, 1887–88) vol. 1, pt. 1, 571.

48 Fiona K. Bellerive, "Uncovering the Exodus: Maritime Women and the Journey to Lowell, Massachusetts, 1860–1880" (undergraduate honours thesis, Mount St Vincent University, 1993), 47.

49 For a discussion of the transformation of the workforce from single, native-born women to immigrant families, see Thomas Dublin, *Women at Work: The Transformation of Work and Community in Lowell, Massachusetts, 1826–1860* (New York: Columbia University Press, 1979). There are numerous historical studies of mill towns in the second half of the nineteenth century and the immigrant communities that lived and worked there. Among those on Massachusetts towns are: Frances H. Early, "French Canadian Beginnings in an American Community: Lowell, Massachusetts, 1868–1886" (PhD diss., Concordia University, 1979); Paul Haebler, "Habitants in Holyoke: The Development of the French Canadian Community in a Massachusetts City, 1865–1910" (PhD diss., University of New Hampshire, 1976).

50 Mary Blewett, *Men, Women and Work: Class, Gender, and Protest in the New England Shoe Industry, 1780–1910* (Urbana: University of Illinois Press, 1988), 343.

51 Edith Abbott, *Women in Industry: A Study in American Economic History* (New York: D. Appleton, 1910; reprint New York: Arno and the New York Times, 1969), 173.

52 Ibid., 336–9.

53 Betsy Beattie, "'Going Up to Lynn': Single, Maritime-Born Women in Lynn, Massachusetts, 1879–1930," *Acadiensis* 22, no. 1 (autumn 1992): 70.

54 Louise Tilly and Joan Scott, *Women, Work, and Family* (New York: Holt, Rinehart and Winston, 1978), 104–5.

CHAPTER TWO

1 The figure of 4,166 women is an underestimate because several pages of the census were illegible and in several districts the census takers merely listed "British Provinces" or "Canada." However, within the entire census for Boston in 1880, the numbers missing are too few to be

statistically significant. See US Census of Population, 1880, Schedule no. 1: Boston, Suffolk County, Massachusetts, in US National Archives and Records Service, *Tenth Census of the United States, 1880* (Washington: NARS, 1960), reels 552–62.

2 These and all subsequent statistics on single, Maritime-born women in Boston are taken from the US Census of Population, ibid. Figures are based on the total number of these women rather than a statistical sample.

3 US Census Office, *Tenth Census (1880)*, 3 vols (Washington: Government Printing Office, 1883), 1:210.

4 Oscar Handlin, *Boston's Immigrants, 1780–1865: A Study in Acculturation* (Cambridge: Harvard University Press, 1941), 80.

5 Ibid., 82–6.

6 Sam Bass Warner, *Streetcar Suburbs: The Process of Growth in Boston, 1870–1900*, 2nd ed. (Cambridge: Harvard University Press, 1978), 6.

7 Most scholars argue that it was not until the 1890s that Boston felt the full impact of southern and eastern European immigration to the city. Sam Bass Warner, for example, writes, "Beginning around 1890, Jews and Italians became an important element in the population of the city." Oscar Handlin, in his study of Boston's immigrants to 1865, does not mention any such migrants. However, in my perusal of the 1880 nominal census for Boston I found pockets of Italians and Portuguese, along with the Irish and Germans who had come in earlier migration streams. See Warner, *Streetcar Suburbs*, 6; Handlin, *Boston's Immigrants*.

8 Massachusetts Bureau of Statistics of Labor, *Census of the Commonwealth of Massachusetts, 1905*, 4 vols (Boston: Wright & Potter, 1908–10), 1:815–16.

9 Warner, *Streetcar Suburbs*, passim.

10 Walter Muir Whitehill, *Boston: A Topographical History*, 2nd ed. (Cambridge: Belknap Press of Harvard University Press, 1968), 141–73.

11 Ibid., passim.

12 Alan Alexander Brookes, "The Exodus: Migration from the Maritime Provinces to Boston during the Second Half of the Nineteenth Century" (PhD diss., University of New Brunswick, 1978), 135.

13 Ibid., 122.

14 Edgar McKay (Alice Peck's son), interview with the author, 5 May 1986.

15 Arthur L. Johnson, "Boston and the Maritimes: A Century of Steam Navigation" (PhD diss., University of Maine, 1971), 2, 11.

16 *The Boston Directory, 1878* (Boston: Sampson, Davenport, 1878), 1192.

17 Johnson, "Boston and the Maritimes," 2.

18 Letter from Margaret Vail Neal to Neil Sinclair, 30 October 1931. A copy of this letter was sent from Neil Sinclair to the author.

19 Elizabeth Wilson, *Fifty Years of Association Work among Young Women, 1866–1916* (New York: National Board of the Young Women's Christian Association of the United States of America, 1916), 32.

20 For a detailed discussion of the important role that the YWCA played in helping young Maritime women to find employment in the late nineteenth and early twentieth centuries see Fiona Bellerive's "Light upon the Shadows of Exodus: Maritime Women and the Boston YWCA, 1890–1910" (Masters thesis, Dalhousie University, 1994).

21 Ibid., 63.

22 Ibid., 69.

23 Wilson, *Fifty Years of Association Work*, 32.

24 Bellerive, "Light upon the Shadows," 68.

25 *Evening Transcript* (Boston), 15 July 1878.

26 Faye E. Dudden, in *Serving Women: Household Service in Nineteenth-Century America* (Middletown, CT: Wesleyan University Press, 1983), noted that for employers "ads were an inconvenience. Placing an ad meant interviewing a stream of girls in one's own home. When her ad appeared, Susan Brown Forbes, of Boston, saw nine applicants the first day and several more the next." Dudden added, "Many prospective domestics placed no ads because they had no homes in which to receive mail or visitors, or because they were illiterate and could not prepare an ad at all" (79).

27 According to statistics from the US Census for 1880, the 7,172 Irish working as servants in Boston represented the largest single nationality in domestic service. While this figure includes men as well as women, it is likely that the vast majority of these servants were women, because women outnumbered men in domestic service by a ratio of over 15 to 1. See US Census Office, *Tenth Census (1880)*, 1:864.

28 *Evening Transcript* (Boston), 15 August 1878.

29 Carol Lasser, "The Domestic Balance of Power: Relations between Mistress and Maid in Nineteenth-Century New England," *Labor History* 28, no. 1 (winter 1987): 17.

30 David M. Katzman, *Seven Days a Week: Women and Domestic Service in Industrializing America* (New York: Oxford University Press, 1978), 101.

31 *Boston City Directory, 1878*, 1013.

32 Katzman, *Seven Days a Week*, 101.

33 Lasser, "The Domestic Balance of Power," 17.

34 Katzman, *Seven Days a Week*, 103–4.

35 Dudden, *Serving Women*, 1.

36 Katzman, *Seven Days a Week*, 53.

37 Ibid., 223.

38 In 1881 Carroll Wright, a labour statistician, gathered information on the living and working conditions of single women in Boston. He noted that "girls living away from home, in boarding and lodging

houses, the latter especially, are often times obliged to practice very close economy in living, one girl being reported as taking her meals at restaurants, and often going without her supper as well as other meals; another as going without meat for weeks, eating bread only without butter, and seldom able to buy a baker's pie." He also mentioned a case where three sisters lived in a single room. See Carroll Wright, *The Working Girls of Boston* (Boston: Wright and Potter, 1889; reprint New York: Arno and the New York Times, 1969), 114.

39 Katzman, *Seven Days a Week*, 139.

40 Ibid., 228.

41 Ibid., 113–14.

42 Ibid., 44.

43 Alice Kessler-Harris, *Out to Work: A History of Wage-Earning Women in the United States* (New York: Oxford University Press, 1978), 135.

44 Daniel Sutherland, *Americans and Their Servants: Domestic Service in the United States from 1800 to 1920* (Baton Rouge: Louisiana State University Press, 1981), 110.

45 Suzanne Sinké, "A Historiography of Immigrant Women in the Nineteenth and Early Twentieth Centuries," *Ethnic Forum* 9, nos 1–2 (1989): 125; Hasia Diner, *Erin's Daughters in America: Irish Immigrant Women in the Nineteenth Century* (Baltimore: Johns Hopkins University Press, 1983), 80–4; Dudden, *Serving Women*, 60–1.

46 Diner, *Erin's Daughters*, 71; Dudden, *Serving Women*, 61.

47 Louise A. Tilly and Joan Scott, *Women, Work, and Family* (New York: Holt, Rinehart and Winston, 1978), 108–9.

48 Wright, *The Working Girls of Boston*, 109.

49 Ibid.

50 Diner, *Erin's Daughters*, 80.

51 Wright, *The Working Girls of Boston*, 79.

52 Carolyn Daniel McCreesh, *Women in the Campaign to Organize Garment Workers, 1880–1917* (New York: Garland Publishing, 1985), 17:

53 Ibid., 77–9.

54 *Globe* (Boston), 18 July 1878.

55 *Evening Transcript* (Boston), 15 August 1878.

56 Mark Peel, "On the Margins: Lodgers and Boarders in Boston, 1860–1900," *Journal of American History* 72, no. 4 (March 1986): 818.

57 Wright, *The Working Girls of Boston*, 114.

58 John Modell and Tamara Hareven, "Urbanization and the Malleable Household: An Examination of Boarding and Lodging in American Families," *Journal of Marriage and the Family* 35, no. 3 (August 1973): 470.

59 Joan W. Scott and Louise A. Tilly, "Women's Work and the Family in Nineteenth-Century Europe," *Comparative Studies in Society and History* 17 (1975): 52–3.

60 Katzman, *Seven Days a Week*, 114.

61 Wright, *Working Girls of Boston*, 53.

62 US Census of Population, 1880, Schedule no. 1: Boston, Suffolk County, Massachusetts, reels 552–62.

63 Letter from Margaret Vail Neal to Neil Sinclair, 30 October 1931.

64 Gary Burrill, *Away: Maritimers in Massachusetts, Ontario, and Alberta: An Oral History of Leaving Home* (Montreal: McGill-Queen's University Press, 1992), 98.

65 Wright, *The Working Girls of Boston*, 99–101.

66 Letter from Margaret Vail Neal to Neil Sinclair, 30 October 1931.

67 Edgar McKay (son of Alice Peck), interview with the author, 5 May 1986.

68 Letter from Mary A. Sheldon, West Newton, Massachusetts, to Lillian Wentzel, Upper Foster Settlement, Nova Scotia, 25 September 1905.

69 *Record* (Kings County, NB), 25 October 1889.

70 "A Visit with Nan Morrison, Baddeck," *Cape Breton's Magazine* no. 47: 12.

71 This anecdote was related to me while I was doing research at the Provincial Archives of New Brunswick in May 1987. The man wished to remain anonymous and to keep the town of his, and the young woman's, birth secret as well. While there was no way to verify the story, the similarity of the facts to other cases of single mothers from the Maritimes suggested that it was true.

72 Barbara Meil Hobson, "Sex in the Marketplace: Prostitution in an American City, Boston, 1820–1880" (PhD diss., Boston University, 1982), 101.

73 Wright, *Working Girls of Boston*, 125–6.

74 Ibid., 124.

75 William Sanger, paraphrased in Hobson, *Sex in the Marketplace*, 130.

76 Ibid.

77 Ibid., 169.

CHAPTER THREE

1 Information on the life of Jennie May Peck Parker is taken from her interview with the author, Bear River, Nova Scotia, 27 May 1989.

2 L.D. McCann, "The Mercantile-Industrial Transition in the Metal Towns of Pictou County, 1857–1931," *Acadiensis* 10, no. 2 (spring 1981): 32; L.D. McCann, "Metropolitanism and Branch Businesses in the Maritimes, 1881–1931," *Acadiensis* 13, no. 1 (autumn 1983): 117.

3 T. William Acheson, "The National Policy and the Industrialization of the Maritimes, 1880–1910," *Acadiensis* 1, no. 2 (spring 1972): 3.

4 McCann, "Metropolitanism and Branch Businesses," 117.

5 James D. Frost, "The 'Nationalization' of the Bank of Nova Scotia, 1880–1910," in T.W. Acheson, David Frank, and James D. Frost, *Industrialization and Underdevelopment in the Maritimes, 1880–1930* (Toronto: Garamond Press, 1985), 53.

6 David Frank, "The Cape Breton Coal Industry and the Rise and Fall of the British Empire Steel Corporation," *Acadiensis* 7, no. 1 (autumn 1977): 3–34.

7 D.A. Muise, "The Industrial Context of Inequality: Female Participation in Nova Scotia's Paid Labour Force, 1871–1921," *Acadiensis* 20, no. 2 (spring 1991): 21.

8 Acheson, "The National Policy," 16–18; Ginette Lafleur, "L'industrialisation et le travail rémuneré des femmes: Moncton, 1881–1891," in *Moncton 1871–1929*, ed. Daniel Hickey (Moncton: Éditions d'Acadie, 1990), 76; Douglas D. Pond, *The History of Marysville, New Brunswick* (Fredericton: the Author, 1983), 28–31; Peter DeLottinville, "The St Croix Cotton Manufacturing Company and Its Influence on the St Croix Community, 1880–1892" (Masters thesis, Dalhousie University, 1979), 306.

9 Larry McCann, "The 1890s: Fragmentation and the New Social Order," in *The Atlantic Provinces in Confederation*, ed. E.R. Forbes and D.A. Muise (Toronto: University of Toronto Press, 1993), 138.

10 Muise, "The Industrial Context," 23; Judith Fingard, "The 1880s: Paradoxes of Progress," in *The Atlantic Provinces in Confederation*, ed. Forbes and Muise, 87.

11 Colin Howell, "The 1900s: Industry, Urbanization, and Reform," in *The Atlantic Provinces in Confederation*, ed. Forbes and Muise, 164.

12 *Sixth Census of Canada, 1921*, 5 vols (Ottawa: F.A. Acland, 1924), 1:342; *Seventh Census of Canada, 1931*, 13 vols (Ottawa: J.O. Patenaude, 1936), 8:44, 74, 144, 365.

13 Claudette Lacelle, *Urban Domestic Servants in 19th-Century Canada* (Ottawa: Environment Canada – Parks, 1987), 137; *Census of Canada, 1880–81*, 3 vols (Ottawa: Maclean, Roger, 1882–85), 1:406, 2:241; *Seventh Census of Canada, 1931*, 13 vols (Ottawa: J.D. Patenaude, 1936–42), 2:157, 7:743–5.

14 *Census of Canada, 1880–81*, 2:253; *Seventh Census of Canada, 1931*, 2:751–7.

15 Muise, "The Industrial Context of Inequality," 16.

16 *Daily News* (Amherst, NS), 6 June 1907.

17 Alison Prentice, in her article on the teaching profession in Canada, dates the feminization of the field to the third quarter of the nineteenth century. See Alison Prentice, "The Feminization of Teaching in British North America and Canada, 1845–1875," *Histoire sociale/Social History* 8 (May 1975): 6.

18 Howell, "The 1900s," 174–5.

19 Many social institutions such as hospitals and reform schools had been established in Maritime cities in the late nineteenth century. However, the first years of the twentieth century – the years of progressive reform – witnessed an upsurge in concern to mitigate the depredations of life in the rapidly growing cities of the region. Led by middle-class reformers, often women, and rooted in a faith in what were believed to be scientific principles, these reforms often translated into a process of isolating vulnerable – and undesirable groups – from the rest of society. The belief in the benefits of segregation led in particular to support for such institutions as homes for the feeble-minded and reform schools for delinquent children. See Judith Fingard, "The 1880s," 107–8; Howell, "The 1900s," 185–6.

20 For a discussion of the feminization of office work in Canada, see Graham S. Lowe, "Class, Job, and Gender in the Canadian Office," *Labour/Le Travailleur* 10 (1982): 11–37.

21 Muise, "The Industrial Context of Inequality," 13.

22 According to Susan Porter Benson, in *Counter Cultures: Saleswomen, Managers, and Customers in American Department Stores, 1890–1940* (Urbana: University of Illinois Press, 1986), by 1890 a "new system of retailing," featuring an "unprecedented combination of size and variety," had been established in the United States. These "department stores" were based on the idea that economies of scale in retailing and "novel appeals to customers" were the twin routes to profits. The principles of variety and size in retailing influenced smaller establishments as well, as exemplified by F.W. Woolworth's Five and Ten Cent stores (14–15).

23 Alison Prentice, Paula Bourne, Gail Cuthbert Brandt, Beth Light, Wendy Mitchinson, and Naomi Black, *Canadian Women: A History* (Toronto: Harcourt Brace Jovanovich, 1988), 128.

24 Muise, "The Industrial Context of Inequality," 16.

25 McCann, "Metropolitanism and Branch Businesses," 118.

26 Michele Martin, *"Hello Central?" Gender, Technology, and Culture in the Formation of Telephone Systems* (Montreal: McGill-Queen's University Press, 1991), 54–6.

27 Muise, "The Industrial Context of Inequality," 15.

28 Ibid., 20.

29 Phillip A. Buckner, "The 1870s: Political Integration," in *The Atlantic Provinces in Confederation*, ed. Forbes and Muise, 59.

30 Andrew Hill Clark summarized the economy of Prince Edward Island in the following description: "The island is still, today, in the twentieth century, the 'million-acre farm' it was eighty years ago." See Andrew Hill Clark, *Three Centuries and the Island: A Historical Geography of Settlement and Agriculture in Prince Edward Island, Canada* (Toronto: University of Toronto Press, 1959), 121.

31 Robert MacKinnon, "Agriculture and Rural Change in Nova Scotia, 1851–1951" (unpublished manuscript), 11.

32 According to 1931 census figures, the total population of the Maritime provinces was 1,009,103, of which 628,124 lived in rural areas and 380,979 lived in urban areas. (The 1931 census defined urban area as all incorporated towns, cities, and villages regardless of size.) See *Seventh Census of Canada, 1931*, 1:154, 365.

33 Ibid., 8:44, 74, 144.

34 Robert MacKinnon, "A Century of Farming in Nova Scotia: The Geography of Agriculture, 1851–1951" (paper presented to the Atlantic Canada Workshop, Fredericton, 25 September 1986), 15.

35 By 1931 the difference in ownership of farm machinery between Maritime farmers and those in the Canadian Prairies was striking. For example, there were 863 tractors on farms in the three Maritime provinces, while farmers in Manitoba alone had 12,983 such machines. See *Seventh Census of Canada, 1931*, 8:lxvii–lxviii.

36 MacKinnon, "A Century of Farming," 9–12.

37 Clark, *Three Centuries and the Island*, 155.

38 *Seventh Census of Canada, 1931*, 8:cxix.

39 MacKinnon, "A Century of Farming," 13.

40 Margaret Conrad, "Apple Blossom Time in the Annapolis Valley, 1880–1957," *Acadiensis* 8, no. 2 (spring 1980): 18–20.

41 L.D. McCann, "'Living a Double-Life': Town and Country in the Industrialization of the Maritimes," in *Geographical Perspectives on the Maritime Provinces*, ed. Douglas Day (Halifax: St Mary's University, 1988), 98.

42 *Seventh Census of Canada, 1931*, 8:56, 89, 159.

43 Danny Sampson, "Dependence and Rural Industry: Inverness, Nova Scotia, 1899–1915" (unpublished manuscript based on a paper given at the Atlantic Canada Workshop, Carleton University, Ottawa, August 1992), 28–9.

44 Muise, "The Industrial Context of Inequality," 12.

45 Louise A. Tilly and Joan W. Scott, *Women, Work, and Family* (New York: Holt, Rinehart and Winston, 1978), 104–45.

46 Tracing single women in Boston back to their parental families in the Maritimes was a thoroughly unscientific process that differed in method depending upon the province of origin and was impossible to do for those from New Brunswick. For Prince Edward Island, the process involved checking women's names on baptismal records, which included place of birth and father's occupation. For Nova Scotia, the procedure involved searching women's birth records. In all cases, records were incomplete, and it was impossible to sort out women with common names, like Mary MacDonald or Annie Gillis, to figure

out which had migrated to Boston. Therefore information about the 292 women who could be traced back to a family, while suggestive, can not be assumed to be representative of all Maritime women in Boston in 1900 and 1910.

47 MacKinnon, "Agriculture and Rural Change," figure 8, Farming zones in Nova Scotia.

48 Clark, *Three Centuries and the Island*, 152.

49 *Casket* (Antigonish, NS), 26 February 1986.

CHAPTER FOUR

1 Information about Lulu Pearl Dempsey taken from a letter from her grandson Robbie Breckenridge of Bathurst, New Brunswick, December 1988, and from the United States manuscript census of 1910 for Boston. See US Census of Population, 1910, Schedule no. 1: Boston, Suffolk County, Massachusetts, in US National Archives and Records Service, *Thirteenth Census of the United States, 1910* (Washington: NARS, 1982), reels 614–26.

2 Information on Anita Saunders Campbell taken from her interview with the author in Weston, Massachusetts, 14 January 1989.

3 Material on Rhoda Gertrude Hyson taken from an information sheet filled out by Kenneth Paulson in 1989; material on Louise Elizabeth Spidell taken from a letter and information sheet filled out by Mrs E. Elliot Brown, Chatham, Massachusetts, in November 1988; material on Esther Campbell taken from a letter and information sheet filled out by Mrs Carol A. Smith in January 1989.

4 Charles H. Trout, *Boston, the Great Depression, and the New Deal* (New York: Oxford University Press, 1977), 4–7.

5 Ibid., Walter Muir Whitehill, *Boston: A Topographical History* (Cambridge: Belknap Press of Harvard University Press, 1968), 187.

6 Frederick A. Bushee, "Ethnic Factors in the Population of Boston," *Publications* of the American Economic Association, 3rd ser., 4, no. 2 (May 1903): 15–16.

7 Massachusetts, Bureau of Statistics, *The Decennial Census, 1915* (Boston: Wright and Potter, 1918), 334.

8 Bushee, "Ethnic Factors," 10.

9 US Census of Population, 1910, Schedule no. 1: Boston, Suffolk County, Massachusetts, reels 614–26; US Census of Population, 1920, Schedule no. 1: Boston, Suffolk County, Massachusetts, in US National Archives and Records Service, *Fourteenth Census of the United States, 1920* (Washington: NARS, 1992), reels 728–43.

10 Ian McKay, "The 1910s: The Stillborn Triumph of Progressive Reform," in *The Atlantic Provinces in Confederation*, ed. E.R. Forbes and D.A. Muise (Toronto: University of Toronto Press, 1993), 226.

11 David Frank, "The 1920s: Class and Region, Resistance and Accommodation" in ibid., 234.

12 Albert J. Kennedy, "'The Provincials,' with an Introduction by Alan A. Brookes," *Acadiensis* 4, no. 2 (spring 1975): 94.

13 Ibid.

14 Susan M. Reverby, *Ordered to Care: The Dilemma of American Nursing, 1850–1945* (Cambridge: Cambridge University Press, 1987), 80.

15 This anecdote was related in an interview with Mary Ross Monroe Hart of North East Margaree, Nova Scotia, 30 May 1989.

16 *Evening Transcript* (Boston), various issues, August 1878.

17 Ibid., 1 July 1910.

18 Ibid., 2 July 1910.

19 Statistics on female Maritime domestics in Ward 11 in 1880, English Canadians in Ward 11 in 1910, and English Canadians in Ward 8 were taken from data collected from the United States manuscript censuses for Boston in 1880, 1910, and 1920 respectively. The number of live-in servants was calculated by subtracting the number of day servants from the total figures for the occupational field of domestic service. See tables B.1 and B.2 in appendix B.

20 David M. Katzman, *Seven Days a Week: Women and Domestic Service in Industrializing America* (New York: Oxford University Press, 1978), 95. Information on the number of female servants in Boston taken from the 1910 and 1920 US censuses. See US Census Office, *Thirteenth Census (1910)* (Washington: Government Printing Office, 1911–14), 4:164; US Census Office, *Fourteenth Census (1920)* (Washington: Government Printing Office, 1921–23), 4:149.

21 As one example of the impact of new household technology on the decline of live-in servants, David Katzman quotes a New England doctor's wife. "'I use a gas range, a fireless cooker, have an excellent vacuum cleaner, and an adequate supply of all kitchen utensils and conveniences,' she wrote. 'My household expenses have been cut down about five hundred dollars a year, and I know of no easier way of saving that amount than by being free from the care and annoyance of a maid.'" Katzman, *Seven Days a Week*, 256.

22 Jacqueline Jones, in her study of African-American women and work, writes that "between 1916 and 1921 an estimated half million blacks, or about 5 percent of the total southern black population, headed north." See Jacqueline Jones, *Labor of Love, Labor of Sorrow: Black Women, Work, and the Family from Slavery to the Present* (New York: Vintage Books, 1986), 156.

23 Ibid., 165.

24 Fiona Bellerive, "Light upon the Shadow of Exodus: Maritime Women and the Boston YWCA, 1890–1910" (Masters thesis, Dalhousie University, 1994), 83–4.

25 H.B. Smith, Certificate of Recommendation for Lillian J. Wentzel, Banks/Baker Manuscript Collection, vol. 2783, no. 2, Public Archives of Nova Scotia, Halifax.

26 Letter, Marion Sheldon, West Newton, Massachusetts, to Lillian Wentzel, Upper Foster Settlement, Nova Scotia, 6 May 1905, ibid., vol. 2783, no. 11.

27 In the 2 July 1910, Boston *Evening Transcript* alone there were nine "Situations Wanted" listings by Swedish women seeking domestic positions. One such ad: "Cook. First Class Swedish cook wants situation where kitchen is kept. Excellent references. Mrs. A. Benson, 89 Pleasant Street."

28 Gary Burrill, *Away: Maritimers in Massachusetts, Ontario, and Alberta: An Oral History of Leaving Home* (Montreal: McGill-Queen's University Press, 1992), 60.

29 Rena Annie MacDonald, interview with the author, Wolfville, Nova Scotia, 3 January 1989.

30 Burrill, *Away*, 61.

31 Letter from Mrs Carol A. Smith, January 1989.

32 Ibid.

33 Information on the number of hospital-based nursing programs in Canada in 1909 taken from Sarah Jane Growe, *Who Cares? The Crisis in Canadian Nursing* (Toronto: McClelland and Stewart, 1991), 48.

34 Letter of Application to Boston City Hospital School of Nursing from Isabel Atkinson of Pictou, Nova Scotia, 1911, Boston City Hospital Training School Records, Nursing Archives, Mugar Library, Boston University.

35 Reverby, *Ordered to Care*, 3.

36 Ibid., 61–2.

37 "With Lottie Morrison from Gabarus," *Cape Breton's Magazine*, no. 40: 7–8.

38 Ibid., 9.

39 Reverby, *Ordered to Care*, 13–21.

40 Ibid., 22.

41 Ibid.

42 For a full explication of the evolution of nurse-training programs see Reverby, *Ordered to Care*, 39–59. A shorter description appears in Barbara Melosh, *"The Physician's Hand": Work Culture and Conflict in American Nursing* (Philadelphia: Temple University Press, 1982), 29–33.

43 Reverby, *Ordered to Care*, 65.

44 Burrill, *Away*, 65.

45 Reverby, *Ordered to Care*, 83.

46 Ibid.

47 Ibid., 79.

48 Records of the Boston City Hospital Training School for Nurses, Nursing Archives, Mugar Library, Boston University.

49 Reverby, *Ordered to Care*, 81–2.

50 David L. Brown and James J. Zuiches, "New England's Population in Historical Perspective," in *The Structure and Impact of Population Redistribution in New England*, ed. Thomas E. Steahr and A.E. Luloff (University Park, PA: Northeast Regional Center for Rural Development, Pennsylvania State University, 1985), 26–7.

51 Bellerive, "Light upon the Shadows," 86–7.

52 *Herald* (Halifax), 17 September 1927; Anita Campbell, interview with the author, Weston, Massachusetts, 14 January 1989.

53 *Herald* (Halifax), 17 September 1927.

54 Interview with Anita Campbell.

55 Information on Edith Isabel Cox taken from author's interview with Mary McSwain Cox and Helen Cox, Charlottetown, Prince Edward Island, 11 July 1989.

56 Information on Marian Oulton taken from a letter and questionnaire filled out by her niece, Mrs Glenn Dobson of Moncton, New Brunswick, in November 1988.

57 Information on fathers' occupations of nursing students taken from the following sources: for Annie Lovett MacDonald, daughter of a mine manager, Burrill, *Away*, 63; for Katherine Inglis, daughter of a dairy farmer, the Antigonish *Casket*, 26 February 1986; for Mable Rainnie, daughter of a manager of a Western Union office, questionnaire filled out by Mrs Glen Dobson, November 1988; and for Martha Ada and Ethel Marguerite Chute, daughters of a gardener/labourer, letter and questionnaire filled out by their nephew Carroll Snell, February 1989.

58 Information on Vera Marina Wotton taken from a questionnaire filled out by her great-nephew William M. Weiler, of Belmont, Massachusetts, December 1989. Information on Louise Elizabeth Spidell taken from a letter written by her daughter Mrs E. Elliott Brown, of Chatham, Massachusetts, in November 1988.

59 Margery W. Davies, *Woman's Place Is at the Typewriter: Office Work and Office Workers, 1870–1930* (Philadelphia: Temple University Press, 1982), 55–61.

60 Louise Marion Bosworth, *The Living Wage of Women Workers: A Study of Incomes and Expenditures of 450 Women in the City of Boston* (New York: Longmans, Green, 1911), 16.

61 Davies, *Woman's Place*, 64–5.

62 Robert A. Woods and Albert J. Kennedy, *Young Working Girls: A Summary of Evidence from Two Thousand Social Workers* (Boston: Houghton Mifflin, 1913), 27.

63 Questionnaire on Vera Wotton filled out by William M. Weiler.
64 Letter from Mrs. E. Elliott Brown.
65 Ibid.
66 Woods and Kennedy, *Young Working Girls*, 22.
67 Carolyn Daniel McCreesh, *Women in the Campaign to Organize Garment Workers, 1880–1917* (New York: Garland Publishing, 1985), 20–1.
68 Ibid., 179–80.
69 Woods and Kennedy, *Young Working Girls*, 24.
70 The number of waitresses for 1910 and 1920 represents the total employees in all types of waitress work mentioned by single English-Canadian women in Boston in each decade. See tables B.2 and B.1 in appendix B for listings by each type of waitress.
71 Dorothy Sue Cobble, *Dishing It Out: Waitresses and Their Unions in the Twentieth Century* (Urbana: University of Illinois Press, 1991), 20.
72 Ibid., 20–2.
73 Alfred Benedict Wolfe, *The Lodging House Problem in Boston* (Cambridge: Harvard University Press, 1913), 28.
74 Cobble, *Dishing It Out*, 36–7.
75 Information on the domiciles of single English-Canadian waitresses in 1910 and 1920 is based on a cross-tabulation of nominal census figures on occupation of these women by the ward in which they lived. See US Census of Population, 1910, Schedule no. 1: Boston, Suffolk County, Massachusetts, reels 614–26; US Census of Population, 1920 Schedule no. 1: Boston, Suffolk County, Massachusetts, reels 728–43.

CHAPTER FIVE

1 Mary Ross Monroe Hart, interview with the author, 30 May 1989, North East Margaree, Nova Scotia.
2 Information on Vera Marina Wotton taken from a letter to the author and a questionnaire filled out by her great-nephew William M. Weiler, of Belmont, Massachusetts, December 1989.
3 Information on Ethel Marguerite Chute taken from a letter to the author and questionnaire filled out by her nephew Carroll Snell, February 1989.
4 Anita Saunders Campbell, interview with the author, 14 January 1989, Weston, Massachusetts.
5 According to Helen Cox, her mother, Edith, who went to Boston to train for nursing, claimed that "everyone went to Boston – it was the thing to do." Letter from Helen Cox to the author, 8 January 1989.
6 Questionnaire filled out by Carroll Snell, February 1989.
7 Mary McSwain Cox, interview with the author, 11 July 1989, Charlottetown, Prince Edward Island.

8 David Weale, *Them Times* (Charlottetown: Institute of Island Studies, 1992), 84.

9 This quotation taken from a longer draft version of the CBC program "Stuck Home" in the possession of David Weale, Charlottetown, Prince Edward Island.

10 Lucile Eaves, *The Food of Working Women in Boston: An Investigation by the Department of Research, Women's Educational and Industrial Union, Boston* (Boston: Wright and Potter, 1917), 167.

11 Massachusetts, Bureau of Statistics of Labor, *The Decennial Census 1915* (Boston: Wright and Potter, 1918), 318–20.

12 Mary McSwain Cox, interview with the author, 11 July 1989, Charlottetown, Prince Edward Island.

13 Albert Benedict Wolfe, *The Lodging-House Problem in Boston* (Cambridge: Harvard University Press, 1913).

14 Mark Peel, "On the Margins: Lodgers and Boarders in Boston, 1860–1900," *Journal of American History* 72, no. 4 (March 1986): 814.

15 Wolfe, *The Lodging-House Problem*, 47.

16 Ibid., passim. See especially chapters 2 through 5, 11–37.

17 Ibid., passim. See especially chapter 6, 52–66.

18 Ibid., 140–1.

19 Eaves, *The Food of Working Women in Boston*, 167.

20 Wolfe, *The Lodging-House Problem*, 103.

21 Ibid., 52.

22 Robert A. Woods, *The City Wilderness: A Settlement Study by Residents and Associates of the South End House* (Boston: Houghton Mifflin, 1898), 49.

23 Wolfe, *The Lodging-House Problem*, 82.

24 For a discussion of the lodging-house subculture, see Peel, "On the Margins," 823.

25 Wolfe, *The Lodging-House Problem*, 102.

26 Ibid., 28–30.

27 Kathy Peiss, *Cheap Amusements: Working Women and Leisure in Turn-of-the-Century New York* (Philadelphia: Temple University Press, 1986).

28 Wolfe, *The Lodging-House Problem*, 30.

29 Ibid., 140–1.

30 Robert A. Woods and Albert J. Kennedy, *Young Working Girls: A Summary of Evidence from Two Thousand Social Workers* (Boston: Houghton Mifflin, 1913), 108–9.

31 Wolfe, *The Lodging-House Problem*, 31.

32 Ibid.

33 Woods and Kennedy, *Young Working Girls*, 112.

34 Information on Lulu Pearl Dempsey taken from a letter to the author from Robbie Breckenridge of Bathurst, New Brunswick, December 1988.

35 Jennie Peck Parker, interview with the author, 27 May 1989, Bear River, Nova Scotia.

36 Joseph E. Garland, *Boston's Gold Coast: The North Shore, 1890–1929* (Boston: Little, Brown, 1981), 18–21.

37 Jennie Peck Parker, interview with the author. Information on Helen Ross taken from an interview conducted by her grandson, Gary Sanders, in Camden, Maine, in the late 1980s and now in the possession of Betsy Beattie.

38 Information on Eva Aulenback taken from her diary, now owned by Tina Swinnimer of Mahone Bay, Nova Scotia.

39 Announcement, Central Evening High School, quoted in Wolfe, *The Lodging-House Problem*, 113.

40 Ibid.

41 Mary McSwain Cox, interview with the author, 11 July 1989, Charlottetown, Prince Edward Island.

42 Anita Saunders Campbell, interview.

43 Maritime Telegraph and Telephone Company, *Monthly Bulletin* 9, no. 4 (April 1916): 41, Archives, Dalhousie University, Halifax.

44 Ibid., 18, no. 8 (August 1925): 89.

45 Ibid., 19, no. 6 (June 1926): 73.

46 Ibid., 19, no. 4 (April 1926): 44.

47 Letter to the author from Thérèse LeLievre LeBlanc, daughter of Marie LeLievre, Cheticamp, Nova Scotia, December 1988.

48 Ibid.

49 Information on Mary Josephine Waterman taken from a letter written to the author by her daughter, Mrs Josephine Fevens, Bridgewater, Nova Scotia, November 1988.

50 Albert J. Kennedy, "'The Provincials,' with an Introduction by Alan A. Brookes," *Acadiensis* 4, no. 2 (spring 1975): 94.

51 Ibid.

52 Quotation of Harriet Barry included in a letter written to the author by her son, Carroll H. Snell, Riverview, New Brunswick, 26 November 1988.

53 Joanne Meyerowitz, whose book *Women Adrift* chronicled the experience of single female migrants to Chicago in the late nineteenth and early twentieth centuries, noted that "in the nineteenth century writers often used the adjective 'adrift' to describe women who had no family nearby and who were not live-in servants, but the label 'women adrift' was not popularized until a federal report of 1910." See Joanne Meyerowitz, *Women Adrift: Independent Wage Earners in Chicago, 1880–1930* (Chicago: University of Chicago Press, 1988), 145.

54 Louise Tilly and Joan Scott, *Women, Work, and Family* (New York: Holt, Rinehart and Winston, 1978), 186–7.

EPILOGUE

1 The most complete discussion of nativist attitudes in nineteenth- and early twentieth-century America is John Higham's *Strangers in the Land: Patterns of American Nativism, 1860–1925*, 2nd ed. (New Brunswick, NJ: Rutgers University Press, 1988).

2 US Immigration and Naturalization Service, *An Immigrant Nation: United States Regulation of Immigration, 1798–1991* (Washington: Government Printing Office, 1991), 9–12.

3 Ibid., 11.

4 Mary Hart, interview with the author, 30 May 1989, Northeast Margaree, Nova Scotia.

5 Kari Levitt, *Population Movements in the Atlantic Provinces* (Fredericton: Atlantic Provinces Economic Growth Council, 1960), 5.

6 According to Margaret Conrad, 82,000 Maritimers left the region in the 1950s alone. See Margaret Conrad, "The 1950s: The Decade of Development," in *The Atlantic Provinces in Confederation*, ed. E.R. Forbes and D.A. Muise (Toronto: University of Toronto Press, 1993), 384.

7 Mary McSwain Cox, interview with the author, 11 July 1989, Charlottetown, Prince Edward Island.

8 David Weale, for example, argued that outmigration engendered "deep feelings of insecurity, self-doubt, dissatisfaction, and envy" among Prince Edward Islanders who did not leave. See page 7 of the draft version of David Weale's CBC radio program "Stuck Home" in his possession at the University of Prince Edward Island, Charlottetown.

Index